Fodor's POCKET

aruba

S0-AEF-527

fodor's travel publications
new york • toronto • london • sydney • auckland
www.fodors.com

contents

maps

on the road with fodor's

A TRIP TAKES YOU OUT OF YOURSELF. Concerns of life at home completely disappear, driven away by more immediate thoughts—about, say, what marvels will beguile the next day, or where you'll have dinner. That's where Fodor's comes in. We make sure that you know all your options, so that you don't miss something that's around the next bend just because you didn't know it was there. Mindful that the best memories of your trip might have nothing to do with what you came to Aruba to see, we guide you to sights large and small all over the island. You might set out to relax in the sun on Eagle Beach, but back at home you find yourself unable to forget the breathtaking rock formation at Natural Bridge or the caves once inhabited by ancient peoples in Arikok National Park. With Fodor's at your side, serendipitous discoveries are never far away.

About Our Writers

Our success in showing you every corner of Aruba is a credit to our extraordinary writers. Although there's no substitute for travel advice from a good friend who knows your style, our contributors are the next best thing—the kind of people you would poll for travel advice if you knew them.

New York–based **Karen W. Bressler** escaped the northeastern winter to interview local celebrities in Aruba. After clubbing at Café Bahia and dipping her toes in the calm waters of Baby Beach, she set about compiling this exciting guidebook—and updating it for us this year—which she hopes will convey Aruba as "one happy island." Karen has written for *Conde Nast Traveler*, *Self*, *Brides*, *Bridal Guide*, and *Honeymoon* magazines and writes regularly for *Elite Traveler* and *Elements*. She also contributed to *Fodor's Brazil*, *Fodor's Caribbean*, and *Fodor's Israel*. Her own books are *Workout on the Go*, *A Century of Lingerie*, *Yoga Baby*, *DIY Beauty*, *The Hair Bible*, and *The Healthy Hollywood Plan*.

Elise Rosen is a writer and editor in New York who knows her ABCs—Aruba, Bonaire, and Curaçao, that is. Her affinity for these Dutch Caribbean islands has even prompted her to begin studying Papiamento, the local vernacular. She works as a financial editor for an investment bank. Elise's extensive background in journalism includes stints as a reporter for the Associated Press in New York and Los Angeles and as a news producer for NY1, Time Warner's cable station. She has also been a contributor to several books, including *Fodor's Caribbean*, *Fodor's Israel*, *Career Opportunities in Art*, and *America's Elite 1000*.

Suzanne Bressler is a New York City–based writer who helped with additional updating work on this edition of *Fodor's Pocket Aruba* and has contributed to *Elite Traveler* magazine and *Fodor's Caribbean*. Although traveling is a favorite pastime, Suzanne's most recent excursions included running 26.2 miles in the 2003 New York City Marathon. The Antarctica Marathon '05 is next on her list. Suzanne anticipates that her new full-time job with Congressman Anthony Weiner, a mayoral hopeful, will be a journey in itself.

You can rest assured that you're in good hands—and that no property mentioned in the book has paid to be included. Each has been selected strictly on its merits, as the best of its type in its price range.

We'd like to thank everyone at the Aruba Hotel and Tourism Authority, Antonio Leo and the Aruba Tourism Authority, and friendly Aruban Ito Tromp. Thanks also go to Barry and Sheila Weintrob, whose Goodwill Ambassadorships (given to visitors of 20 consecutive years) are just around the corner.

Don't Forget to Write

Your experiences—positive and negative—matter to us. If we have missed or misstated something, we want to hear about it. We follow up on all suggestions. Contact the Aruba editor at editors@fodors.com or c/o Fodor's at 1745 Broadway, New York, NY 10019. And have a fabulous trip!

Tim Jarrell
Publisher

aruba

The small crowd inside the main lounge of the cruise ship, which has just docked this morning, includes government officials and members of the press, on hand to greet passengers of its inaugural voyage. Flashbulbs reflect off newly shined mirrors and bottles of champagne as the captain takes center stage. "I sailed to Aruba every week for almost 25 years, but that was a long time ago. I can't tell you how good it is to be back; now I know I'm home again."

In This Chapter

introducing aruba

FLAIR IS AN ARUBAN HALLMARK— flair for language, music, food, hospitality, storytelling, and, above all, for life. You'll notice this joie de vivre as you meander through the streets or mingle with locals in a bar. Perhaps you'll revel in it as you paint the town red, dine at a fine restaurant, kick back at your hotel, or soak up the sun on a beach. Aruba's slogan sums it up best; this is, indeed, "One Happy Island."

The "A" in the ABC Islands (the other two being Bonaire and Curaçao), tiny Aruba got its name from the Arawak word *oruba* (meaning "well placed"), as it was convenient to the coast of South America. The conquistadors also found it a good jumping-off point for the Spanish Main, which held the promise of great riches. They called the island *oro hubo* ("possessing gold"). There was gold, although it wasn't discovered until many years after the conquistadors first arrived. Today both meanings hold true— Aruba is both a place of golden sunny days and a convenient vacation destination where golden memories are made.

Once a member of the Netherlands Antilles, the island became an independent entity within the Netherlands in 1986. Throughout its history Aruba's economy has relied on trading horses, mining gold (discovered here in 1824), cultivating aloe plants, and refining Venezuelan oil. These days, however, tourism is the primary industry, and the island's population of 71,000 treats visitors as valued guests. The national anthem proclaims, "The greatness of our people is their great cordiality," and this is no exaggeration. Waiters serve you with smiles, English is spoken everywhere, and hotel hospitality directors appear delighted to fulfill your needs.

With its low humidity, average temperature of 28°C (82°F), modest rainfall, and location below the hurricane belt, Aruba seems like paradise. Silky sands and cooling trade winds have made the calm southwest coast a tourist mecca. Most of the island's 28 major hotels—with on-site restaurants, boutiques, and casinos—sit side by side down a single strip of shore. Every night sees theme parties, treasure hunts, beachside barbecues, and fish fries enlivened by steel bands or dancers. Surround all this with warm blue-green waters and you've got the perfect destination for anyone who wants sun salted with lots of activities. Courteous service, efficient amenities, modern casinos, glorious beaches, duty-free shopping, and remarkably varied cuisine help fill Aruba's more than 7,500 hotel rooms.

THE MAKING OF ARUBA

THE PEOPLE

Aruba's first inhabitants were the Caiquetio people of the Arawak tribe (the earliest relics of their existence date from 2500 BC), who migrated from South America to avoid clashes with the more aggressive Caribs. The Arawaks formed a peaceful tribal society, living in small family groups subsisting on fish and making rudimentary tools from shells and stones. As their civilization developed, they turned to farming. Recent excavations in the Santa Cruz area have unearthed remnants of vessel pottery— cooking pots, baking griddles, burial urns, and other finely polished and painted pieces—and fragments of wooden house posts that indicate sophisticated design and manufacturing techniques. Inscriptions from about AD 1000 are still visible in Aruba's limestone caves.

Islandscapes

Aruba's topography is unusual for a Caribbean island. The southern and western coasts consist of miles of palm-lined, white-sand beaches. The calm, blue-green waters are so clear that in some areas visibility extends to a depth of 100 feet. The northeast coast is wild and rugged; here the waves pound against the coral cliffs, creating remarkable rock formations. The desertlike interior is home to various types of cacti and still more extraordinary rock formations. And everywhere, divi-divi trees flourish.

Poking out of the Caribbean Sea, Aruba is at latitude 12°30′ north and longitude 70° west and lies about 32 km (20 mi) from Venezuela's northern coast, near the Península Paraguaná. It's a small island, only 32 km (20 mi) long and 10 km (6 mi) across at its widest point, with a total area of 180 square km (70 square mi).

In the east, Arikok National Park makes up 18% of the island's total area. In the park is the 617-foot Mt. Yamanota, Aruba's highest peak. The capital, Oranjestad, is on the southwest coast. Here Dutch and Spanish influences are evident in the colorful houses along Wilhelminastraat. Two main thoroughfares—J. E. Irausquin and L. G. Smith boulevards—link the capital to the hotels along Eagle and Palm beaches.

To the southeast lies San Nicolas, the island's second-largest metropolis and the site of an oil refinery. At Aruba's northwestern tip are large rolling sand dunes. Nestled at the island's heart, Santa Cruz is the cradle of religious culture, symbolized by a large cross marking the spot where Spanish missionaries introduced Christianity.

In about 1499 Spanish explorer Alonso de Ojeda (a lieutenant of Christopher Columbus) was the first European to land on the island. According to oral history, an Arawak chieftain guided the first Spanish inland, where they erected a cross to mark the occasion. (In 1968 this event was commemorated by the placement of a large wooden cross atop a rocky hill in Santa Cruz.) Believing there were no precious metals, the conquerors exported the entire Arawak population in 1515 to Hispaniola (today's Dominican Republic and Haiti) to work in the copper mines. Though some were allowed to return after 1527, when Spain actively began to colonize Aruba, Bonaire, and Curaçao, the mass abduction ended much of the Arawak culture on the island.

In 1636, during the Eighty Years' War between Holland and Spain, the Dutch took control of Aruba, Bonaire, and Curaçao, ruling them under the charter of the Dutch West India Company. Over the next 100 years, commerce grew on the island, which served as a satellite to the administrative center on larger Curaçao.

Owing to the arid climate and poor soil, Aruba was spared from plantation economics and the slave trade; instead, the Dutch used the remaining Arawaks to herd cattle. The Dutch held power until 1805, when the English laid claim to Aruba briefly during the Napoleonic Wars. The Dutch Republic on the European continent had fallen to the French in 1795, and France annexed the Netherlands in 1810. But after Napoléon's defeat in 1815, political lines throughout Europe were redrawn. The Kingdom of the Netherlands was born, and in 1816 possession of Aruba was returned permanently to the Dutch.

In 1750, Domingo Antonio Silvestre—who had been converted to Catholicism by Spanish missionaries—built a small chapel at Alto Vista on the island's north shore to accommodate the Catholic community, which until this time had had no formal place of worship. The winding approach road is lined with 12 white crosses indicating the stations of the cross, which pilgrims can follow to the tranquil chapel. The church of Santa Ana, built in the district of Noord in 1776, is renowned for its handsomely carved oak altar, which was awarded a prize for neo-Gothic design at the Rome exhibition of 1870.

The first Protestant church was built in 1848 in the center of Oranjestad. Today the original building houses a museum that is maintained by the congregation; an adjoining larger church is used for weekly services. Another landmark house of worship, the Inmaculada Concepción church in Santa Cruz, is noted for the colorful biblical mural decorating its nave. The Beth Israel synagogue was built in 1962 to meet the needs of the growing Jewish community. (A congregation began forming as early as the 1920s, when an international workforce was drawn to Aruba to staff the oil refinery.)

With a history full of cultures clashing and melding, it's no surprise that most islanders are fluent in several languages. School lessons are taught in Dutch, the official language. Arubans begin studying English, recognized as the international tongue, beginning in the fourth grade. Spanish, essential because of Aruba's proximity to South America, is taught in school as early as fifth grade, and French is offered as an option in high school. In normal conversation, however, the locals speak Papiamento—a mix of Spanish, Dutch, Portuguese, English, and French, as well as Indian and African languages. Since 1998, Papiamento has also been taught in grade school.

THE ECONOMY

Early on, Aruba's main source of income was drawn from exporting horses—brought in by the Spanish and bred on the island—to Jamaica and Cuba. In the 16th century, Aruba was a free-roaming horse ranch. There were no European settlements other than garrisons until the 19th century. Later, the island's Arawak population herded cattle that were traded or sold to

Curaçao, and made glass objects to sell. The first white colonists arrived from Curaçao in 1754, and several merchant families followed. Many who settled here in the 18th century worked in Venezuela as seasonal laborers on coffee and cocoa plantations; others headed for Jamaica and Cuba. Then in 1824 the discovery of gold on the island's northern slopes at Rooi Fluit boosted the economy. Intermittent reports of gold finds led several exploration companies to set up shop, until the gold was exhausted and related businesses ceased operations in 1916.

Another major revenue source was the cultivation of aloe (raw sap from the plant was used as a laxative). By the 1920s Aruba was responsible for 70% of the world's aloe supply, with England accounting for most of the intake. The crop brought in about $1 million per year. Calcium phosphate was also a source of income; it was mined in Aruba from 1879 to 1914 and exported to Europe and the United States.

But it was oil that ultimately fueled Aruba's economic boom. In 1924, the Lago refinery was built in San Nicolas. Searching for a hospitable seaport and a stable political climate in which to process the oil from Venezuela's Lake Maracaibo fields, the Standard Oil Company of New Jersey (later Exxon) took over the refinery in 1932. It was soon producing 440,000 barrels of refined oil a day. The company hired thousands of North Americans, Arubans, and other Caribbean islanders, and San Nicolas thrived as residential and commercial areas sprang up to accommodate the workforce.

The refinery played an integral role in World War II, producing one in every 16 gallons of motor fuel used by the Allies. A German submarine had orders to destroy the refinery in 1942 but was unable to fire its cannons. Historians theorize that this failure was one of the events that tipped the hand of victory toward the Allies. By 1949 the refinery employed 8,300 people— roughly 16% of the populace. Indeed, Aruba's population grew sixfold in the three decades after the refinery was built, surging from 9,000 in 1924 to 54,000 in 1954.

Because of an unstable oil market, however, the refinery was closed in 1985. Although the Coastal Corporation of Texas reopened it in 1991 (and it now produces 150,000 barrels a day), the tourist trade has replaced oil as Aruba's primary source of income. Education, health care, and other public services are financed by tourism, which has also helped to keep the unemployment rate at less than 1%. Because of this, it's no surprise that guests are warmly received. This warmth has, in turn, contributed to a general upward trend in the number of visitors—from 206,750 in 1985 to 642,627 in 2002.

THE GOVERNMENT

Until late 1985 Aruba was a member of the Netherlands Antilles, along with Bonaire, Curaçao, St. Maarten, St. Eustatius, and Saba. On January 1, 1986, Aruba was granted a new status as an independent entity within the Kingdom of the Netherlands, which now consists of the Netherlands, the Netherlands Antilles, and Aruba.

The island has a royally appointed governor, who acts as the Dutch sovereign's representative for a six-year term. Executive power is held by the seven-member council of ministers, appointed by the legislative council for four-year terms and presided over by the prime minister, who is elected every four years. The legislature consists of a parliament whose 21 members are elected by popular vote to serve a four-year term. Legal jurisdiction lies with the Common Court of Justice of Aruba and the Netherlands Antilles as well as the Supreme Court of Justice at The Hague in the Netherlands. Defense and foreign affairs still fall under the realm of the kingdom, whereas internal matters involving such things as customs, immigration, aviation, and communications are handled autonomously.

"Go On with the Struggle"

Arubans are proud of their autonomous standing within the Kingdom of the Netherlands, and Gilberto François "Betico" Croes is heralded as the hero behind the island's status aparte (separate status). His birthday, January 25, is an official Aruban holiday.

During the Dutch colonial expansion of the 17th century, Aruba and five other islands—Bonaire, Curaçao, St. Maarten, St. Eustatius, and Saba—became territories known as the Netherlands Antilles. After World War II, these islands began to pressure Holland for autonomy, and in 1954 they became a collective self-governing entity under the umbrella of the Kingdom of the Netherlands.

At that time, several political parties were in power on the island. Soon, however, Juancho Irausquin (who has a major thoroughfare named in his honor) formed a new party that maintained control for nearly two decades. Irausquin was considered the founder of Aruba's new economic order and the forebear of modern Aruban politics. After his death, his party's power diminished.

In 1971 Croes, then a young, ambitious school administrator, became the leader of another political party. Bolstered by a thriving economy generated by Aruba's oil refinery, Croes spearheaded the island's cause to secede from the Netherlands Antilles and to gain status as an equal partner within the Dutch kingdom. Sadly, he didn't live to celebrate the realization of his dream. On December 31, 1985, the day before Aruba's new status became official, Croes was in a car accident that put him in a coma for 11 months. He died on November 26, 1986. Etched in the minds of Arubans are his prophetic words: "Si mi cai na cominda, gara e bandera y sigui cu e lucha" ("If I die along the way, seize the flag and go on with the struggle").

THE LANGUAGE

Papiamento is a unique Creole language—a mellifluous blend of African, European, and Arawak tongues—that's widely spoken on Aruba, Bonaire, and Curaçao. One theory holds that Papiamento originated on Curaçao in the 17th century to afford a means of communication between African slaves and their Dutch owners. Another holds that the language developed somewhat earlier, blending the tongues of the Spanish settlers and the indigenous population. In either case, words and phrases were soon borrowed from still other peoples, including Portuguese and Spanish missionaries and South American traders. Still later, it was peppered with some English and French elements.

Linguists believe the name Papiamento (a variation of Papiamentu) probably derives from the Portuguese verb *papiar*, meaning "to chatter." In Papiamento, as in some other Creole languages, the verb *papia* means "to speak." Add the suffix *mentu*, which means "the way of doing something," and you form a noun. Thus, Papiamento is roughly translated as "the way of speaking." (Sometimes the suffix -*mentu* is spelled in the Spanish and Portuguese way [-*mento*], creating the variant spelling.)

Papiamento began as an oral tradition, handed down through the generations and spoken by all social classes. On Aruba, you'll hear a lilting tone to the language, whereas on Curaçao, the delivery is more rapid-fire. On Bonaire, the sound is somewhere in between. There's no uniform spelling or grammar from island to island or even from one neighborhood to another.

In 1995 Aruba's citizens began a grassroots effort to raise awareness of Papiamento and to have it taught in the schools. It was made part of the curriculum in 1998; that year was also declared the Year of Papiamento on Aruba. With its official recognition, Papiamento continues to be refined and standardized.

Papiamento Primer

Arubans enjoy it when visitors use their language, so don't be shy. You can buy a Papiamento dictionary to build your vocabulary, but here are a few pleasantries—including some terms of friendship and love—to get you started:

BON DIA.	Good morning.
BON TARDI.	Good afternoon.
BON NOCHI.	Good evening/night.
BON BINI.	Welcome.
AJO.	Bye.
TE AWORO.	See you later.
PASA UN BON DIA.	Have a good day.
DANKI.	Thank you.
NA BO ORDO.	You're welcome.
CON TA BAI?	How are you?
MI TA BON.	I am fine.
BAN GOZA!	Let's enjoy!
PABIEN!	Congratulations!
QUANTO COSTA ESAKI?	How much is this?
HOPI BON	Very good
AMI	Me
ABO	You
NOS DOS	The two of us
MI DUSHI	My sweetheart
KU TUR MI AMOR	With all my love
UN BRAZA	A hug
UN SUNCHI	A kiss
RANKA LENGA	To French kiss
MI STIMA ARUBA.	I love Aruba.

PORTRAITS

TOURISM FACES NEW CHALLENGES

Juggling the day-to-day operations of the Aruba Tourism Authority is no easy task, but it's one that Myrna Jansen has mastered. As managing director of the ATA, she works closely with the island's minister of tourism in her efforts to attract more visitors from the United States, Canada, South America, and Europe.

The most challenging part of her job, Jansen says, is working in a world that changed so dramatically on September 11, 2001. After years of steady gains, tourism dipped. This could have been devastating for an island that relies so much on tourism dollars. But her office shifted into high gear, getting out the message that Aruba is a safe and secure destination.

Things are looking up. The number of visitors from the United States in 2003 increased by about 6%; at the same time, the number of visitors from Europe rose by double digits. "We're heading in the right direction," says Jansen, "and it's been very rewarding."

FODOR'S: What makes Aruba a great place to vacation?

JANSEN: It's a great place to live, so it's a great place to visit. The people are always happy and we have a good quality of life, which is reflected on our tourists. We have beautiful and consistent weather; it's always 82 degrees and sunny, which has become more and more important to visitors.

FODOR'S: What do you treasure most about the island?

JANSEN: The people are something we treasure very much. Most of our visitors—about 40 percent—return, and many continue to visit for 30 years. They all say it's the people that make the place. I'm an Aruban and I know our hospitality shows through our interaction with visitors and through the quality of service we offer them. In addition, most Arubans are highly educated, and that brings with it a certain comfort level for visitors.

FODOR'S: Do you have a story of a special encounter with a tourist that has touched your life?

JANSEN: I met one gentleman who has been coming here for over 35 years. He always comes with a group and always stays at the same hotel, where he throws a party every year. When he speaks about why he keeps bringing people back, they are special moments that he shares with me. Also, many visitors tell us about things they feel shouldn't change because that's how they were 30 years ago. It's nice that they feel so strongly about these parts of our culture.

FODOR'S: Do you find that long-term tourists want to give back to the island?

JANSEN: There are visitors who come here and hold fund-raising events for charities like Friends of the Handicapped, which is a foundation started by tourists who wanted to give back to the island. They come every year and raise money for handicapped Arubans. Other visitors have written songs about Aruba and presented us with lyrics and music.

FODOR'S: Where are your favorite places to go on Aruba? What do you on a typical day off?

JANSEN: As a mother of three kids, I spend most of my free time with them. We usually go shopping or go to the beach, which is the most important activity for relaxation with my family. I love the part of Eagle Beach where the beach area is very wide and there are no hotels. One of my favorite sites is the north coast because it's rough and exciting. I don't get there that often, but I enjoy it when I'm there.

FODOR'S: How has Aruba changed over the past two years?

Distance Conversion Chart

KILOMETERS/MILES

To change kilometers (km) to miles (mi), multiply km by .621.

To change mi to km, multiply mi by 1.61.

KM TO MI	MI TO KM
1=.62	1=1.6
2=1.2	2=3.2
3=1.9	3=4.8
4=2.5	4=6.4
5=3.1	5=8.1
6=3.7	6=9.7
7=4.3	7=11.3
8=5.0	8=12.9

METERS/FEET

To change meters (m) to feet (ft), multiply m by 3.28.

To change ft to m, multiply ft by .305.

M TO FT	FT TO M
1=3.3	1=.30
2=6.6	2=.61
3=9.8	3=.92
4=13.1	4=1.2
5=16.4	5=1.5
6=19.7	6=1.8
7=23.0	7=2.1
8=26.2	8=2.4

JANSEN: The only way the island has changed is that we have more activities and new places to sightsee, like the new Carnival Museum, the newly renovated Numismatic Museum, and new art galleries, most of which hold exhibitions every month and other regular events for the public.

FODOR'S: Where do you travel to on vacation and why?

JANSEN: In the past, I've been to Disney World with the kids and to Holland. I find Europe very exciting, and Holland is a gateway to Europe. My kids will go there to study, so it is important for them to feel comfortable there. Sometimes I visit other islands like Curaçao, which is only 20 minutes away, and sometimes I'll take a cruise.

FODOR'S: Describe an Aruban tradition that you cherish.

JANSEN: I cherish Dande. It's a New Year's tradition in which groups of people go from house to house singing songs that are personalized about the people living in each house. When I was very young, it was a big thing at our house and a very emotional moment for my family.

FODOR'S: Is there any message you would like to convey to vacationers about Aruba?

JANSEN: I think that Aruba can be a very active island, but a lot of visitors have the perception that there's not a lot to do here. If you're going to relax, you can always sit on the beach with a piña colada, but there are plenty of other options if you want to be active. The choice is there; it's up to you to decide what to do.

Your Checklist for a Perfect Journey

WAY AHEAD
- Devise a trip budget.
- Write down the five things you want most from this trip. Keep this list handy before and during your trip.
- Make plane or train reservations. Book lodging and rental cars.
- Arrange for pet care.
- Check your passport. Apply for a new one if necessary.
- Photocopy important documents and store in a safe place.

A MONTH BEFORE
- Make restaurant reservations and buy theater and concert tickets. Visit fodors.com for links to local events.
- Familiarize yourself with the local language or lingo.

TWO WEEKS BEFORE
- Replenish your supply of medications.
- Create your itinerary.
- Enjoy a book or movie set in your destination to get you in the mood.

- Develop a packing list. Shop for missing essentials. Repair and launder or dry-clean your clothes.

A WEEK BEFORE
- Stop newspaper deliveries. Pay bills.
- Acquire traveler's checks.
- Stock up on film.
- Label your luggage.
- Finalize your packing list— take less than you think you need.
- Create a toiletries kit filled with travel-size essentials.
- Get lots of sleep. Don't get sick before your trip.

A DAY BEFORE
- Drink plenty of water.
- Check your travel documents.
- Get packing!

DURING YOUR TRIP
- Keep a journal/scrapbook.
- Spend time with locals.
- Take time to explore. Don't plan too much. Sample text.

A yellow-bellied barika geel lands on the table and gazes enviously at the buffet breakfast of muffins, mangoes, and berries. The waves glisten in the background, and the sun lights up his colorful feathers as he flutters impatiently and staggers around, planning his next move. Even the seagulls gliding overhead can't divert the little guy's attention. Someone puts a morsel of food in front of him; he eagerly grabs it before flying off into the warm air of another perfect Aruban day.

In This Chapter

perfect days and nights

ARE YOU PERPLEXED ABOUT WHICH OF ARUBA'S MANY BEACHES is best or about how to spend your time during one of the island's rare rainy days? Below are some suggestions to guide you. There are also a few ideas on how to spend a night (or two) celebrating all the perfect days you've been having.

A PERFECT DAY AT THE BEACH

Aruba's white sands and turquoise waters are legendary, but for perfection, head to the island's southernmost tip, where the beaches are the most secluded. Just make sure you wear plenty of sunscreen; the cooling trade winds can be deceiving.

Before setting out, rent snorkel gear at your hotel so that you can fully appreciate the calm water and all its inhabitants. And why not pack a picnic? Many hotels will prepare one at your request, or you can stop by a supermarket (there are several on L. G. Smith Boulevard) to pick up provisions for the day.

The Kadushi Juice Bar at the foot of the beachfront pool area at the Hyatt Regency Aruba in Palm Beach is a great place to start your day. Slowly sip a fruit or veggie smoothie as you relax on a lounge chair overlooking the waves. From here, make the 27-km (17-mi) trip by rental car southeast to Baby Beach, which is as placid as a wading pool and just about as shallow (only 4–5 feet deep). The shady, thatched areas that dot its powdery sands are ideal for cooling off.

Splash about in the water or do a little snorkeling. Try your hand at a game of paddleball or Frisbee (borrow equipment from your hotel before setting out). In the afternoon, sack out on the sand and get some well-deserved rest. After all, you're on vacation. Be sure to wake up in time to head back for the daily happy hour (4:30–6 PM) at the Sunset Beach Bistro at the Aruba Phoenix Beach Resort in Palm Beach or at the Pelican Nest on Pelican Pier in Palm Beach.

A PERFECT RAINY DAY

Aruba has a reputation for guaranteed sunshine because of its location outside the hurricane belt. But weather patterns can be unpredictable. Here's what to do if you get caught in a storm.

Have breakfast at DeliFrance in the Certified Mega Mall on L. G. Smith Boulevard. The freshly baked bagels and the hot Dutch pancakes covered in powdered sugar will surely warm you up. By 10 or so, head to downtown Oranjestad to see the Archaeological Museum of Aruba, where you'll get a taste of local history from the extensive collection of Arawak artifacts, farm and domestic utensils, and skeletons. Nearby, the Numismatic Museum houses a fascinating collection of rare coins from around the world. Because you'll be in the heart of town, this is a great time to catch the mesmerizing Experience Aruba Panorama, a 22-minute film complete with 3-D effects and surround sound, at the Renaissance Aruba Beach Resort's Crystal Theater. Shows start every hour.

For lunch, head to the pool bar at the Divi Aruba Beach Resort, where the brick oven cooks up some of the island's tastiest pizzas. Make-your-own-daiquiri machines wait for you to fulfill your bartending fantasies. The canopy over the bar will shield you from the rain, and the people on the bar stools beside you will no doubt swap stories (and maybe even drinks) with you while you wait out the weather.

After lunch, it's time to indulge yourself. Try the Mandara Spa at the Marriott Aruba Ocean Club, which offers Swedish, sports-reflexology, and aromatherapy massages, as well as other exotic treatments, such as the exfoliating Bali Coffee Scrub. Your body will thank you. Your soul will, too. Stick around to luxuriate in the spa's mint-oil-scented steam room and pick up a pot of foot balm to carry the experience into your postvacation days. Another option is the Eagle Bowling Palace, which has 16 lanes, a snack bar, and even a cocktail lounge. As you celebrate picking up that spare, you'll never know how frightful the weather is outside. Wrap up your rainy day with an early evening movie at the Seaport Cinema in the Seaport Village Market Place. Its six theaters show the latest blockbusters from Hollywood.

A PERFECT NIGHT OF ROMANCE

When the sun goes down, Aruba becomes one of the most romantic settings on earth. Here's how to share it with that special someone.

Make reservations for cocktails at Brisas del Mar, which is always packed at sunset. Ask for a table on the terrace, where the breeze is inviting and the ocean view is mesmerizing. If you're lucky, the longtime owner will join you for a bit and tell wonderful stories of past guests. Be careful what you say—you may end up in one of these tales.

Or for a magical moment at sunset right on the beach—simultaneously luxurious and laid-back—arrange for a champagne toast at water's edge at the Aruba Marriott Resort & Stellaris Casino. An attendant in a beach-style tux will have the bubbly on ice at your table in the sand, ready to pop the cork just as the sun melts into the horizon. Have dinner at Le Dôme, another place where reservations are required. Service doesn't get any better than this; neither does food. Share a delectable French dish, dive into a dessert for two, order some coffee, and cozy up on the couch in the center of the main dining room.

After dinner, head for the Sirocco Lounge in the Wyndham's Casablanca Casino. Sip a cocktail and listen to live jazz (Thursdays through Saturdays). Or be daring and puff on an authentic Arabian hookah pipe. Later, test your luck at the roulette wheel. Try numbers that have special meaning for you, such as each other's birthday, your wedding anniversary, or the day you met. End the evening with a walk—hand in hand—along the beach.

A PERFECT ALL-NIGHTER

Want to take advantage of everything Aruba has to offer? Here's an action-packed guide of things to do from sundown to sunup.

Check out the Sunset Salute, accompanied by live music, at the Sunset Bar in the Radisson Aruba Caribbean Resort. If you want to dance like the locals, stick around for the merengue lessons.

Make dinner reservations at L'Escale, an upscale eatery overlooking the marina at the Renaissance Aruba Beach Resort & Casino. You'll be serenaded by a Hungarian string trio as the courteous staff caters to your every need. The succulent dishes—fresh mahimahi, Caribbean-style snapper, rich chocolate soufflé—will surely satisfy your appetite.

At 9 PM, check out Let's Go Latin—a dazzling revue of singing and dancing—at the Renaissance's Crystal Theater. Afterward, head to the trendy Garufa Cigar & Cocktail Lounge for live jazz, a cognac, and perhaps a stogie. The chic bar stools are so comfortable you may not want to leave. And besides, the dance floor keeps getting hotter at the next stop, Mambo Jambo, well into the night.

When you just can't dance any longer, head for the 24-hour Crystal Casino, where you can give your feet a break and instead put on your thinking cap at the blackjack table.By sunrise, you should be on the beach—any beach. Afterward sip coffee, scan the local papers (or download international ones), and sink your toes into the sand at MooMba Beach Bar & Restaurant (between the Holiday Inn and the Marriott Surf Club), where you can people-watch over breakfast, beginning at 8 AM.

The restaurant, typically packed with tourists, is now full of locals on an afternoon outing. They're joined at the bar by a visitor from New York who has befriended them to learn more about island life. After a few Balashi beers, the stories flow—tales of "yesterday's soup" (a belief that soup tastes better the second day) and jouvert (a street party that starts at 3 AM and lasts until sunrise to kick off Carnival). When their table is ready, the Arubans invite their new friend along to sample native specialties. The New Yorker hadn't planned to dine on goat stew, but when in Rome . . .

In This Chapter

eating out

THERE ARE A FEW HUNDRED RESTAURANTS ON ARUBA, from elegant eateries to seafront shacks, so you're bound to find something to tantalize your taste buds. You can sample a wide range of cuisines—Italian, French, Argentine, Asian, and Cuban, to name a few—reflecting Aruba's eclectic blend of cultures. Chefs have to be creative on this tiny island, because of the limited number of locally grown ingredients: *maripampoen* (a vegetable that's often stewed with meat and potatoes), *hierba di hole* (a sweet-spicy herb used in fish soup), and *shimaruku* (a fruit similar to the cherry) are among the few.

Although most resorts offer better-than-average dining, don't be afraid to try one of the many excellent independent places. Ask locals about their favorite spots; some of the lesser-known restaurants offer food that's reasonably priced and definitely worth sampling.

Most restaurants on the western side of the island are along Palm Beach or in downtown Oranjestad, both easily accessible by taxi or bus. Some restaurants in Savaneta and San Nicolas are worth the trip; a car is the best way to get there.

To give visitors an affordable way to sample the island's eclectic cuisine, the **Aruba Gastronomic Association** (Rooi Santo 21, Noord, tel. 297/586–2161, 800/477–2896 in U.S., www.arubadining.com) has created a dine-around program involving more than 20 island restaurants. Here's how it works: you can buy tickets for three dinners ($109 per person), five dinners ($177), seven dinners ($245), or five breakfasts or lunches plus four dinners ($214). Dinners include an appetizer, an entrée, dessert, coffee or tea, and a service charge. Other programs, such as gift certificates and coupons for dinners at the association's VIP member restaurants, are available. You can buy dine-around tickets using the association's online order form, through travel agents, or at the De Palm Tours sales desk in many hotels. Participating restaurants change frequently; the AGA Web site has the latest information.

PRICES & DRESS

Aruba's elegant restaurants—where you might have to dress up a little (jackets for men, sundresses for women)—can be pricey. If you want to spend fewer florins, opt for the more casual spots, where being comfortable is the only dress requirement. A sweater draped over your shoulders will go a long way against the chill of air-conditioning. If you plan to eat in the open air, bring along insect repellent in case the mosquitoes get unruly.

CATEGORY	COST*
$$$$	over $30
$$$	$20–$30
$$	$12–$20
$	$8–$12
¢	under $8

*Prices are per person for a main course at dinner, excluding service charges or taxes.

HOW & WHEN

To ensure you get to eat at the restaurants of your choice, make some calls when you get to the island—especially during high season—to secure reservations. If you're heading to a restaurant in Oranjestad for dinner, leave about 15 minutes earlier than you think you should; in-town traffic can become ugly once beach hours are over. Note that on Sunday you may have a hard time finding a restaurant that's open for lunch, and that many eateries are closed for dinner on Sunday or Monday. Breakfast lovers are in luck. For quantity, check out the buffets at the Hyatt, Marriott, or Wyndham resorts or local joints such as DeliFrance.

Argentine

$$–$$$$ **EL GAUCHO ARGENTINE GRILL.** Faux-leather-bound books, tulip-top lamps, wooden chairs, and tile floors decorate this Argentine steak house, which has been in business since 1977. A glass of rich red wine from the extensive cellar and the melt-in-your-mouth garlic bread will tantalize your taste buds as you await your meal. Main dishes include thick *churrasco* (Argentine steak) smothered in peppers and onions. For dessert, go for the *helado argentino* (vanilla ice cream with sweet-potato marmalade and caramel) or the *torta de queso* (otherwise known as cheesecake). *Wilhelminastraat 80, Oranjestad, tel. 297/582–3677, www.elgaucho-aruba.com. AE, D, MC, V. Closed Sun.*

Asian

$$–$$$ **KOWLOON.** In addition to many Chinese provinces, Indonesia is also represented on the menu here. Try the *bami goreng*, a noodle dish with shreds of shrimp, pork, vegetables, and an intoxicating blend of herbs and spices. *Saté* (grilled strips of beef or chicken in a spicy peanut sauce), an assortment of curries, and steak prepared in a variety of ways are also available. The modern Asian decor blends well with the island's palms and sands. *Emmastraat 11, Oranjestad, tel. 297/582–4950. AE, MC, V.*

Chowing Down Aruban Style

The finest restaurants require at the most only a jacket for men and a sundress for women. Still, after a day on the beach, even this might feel formal. For a truly casual bite, visit one of Aruba's ice cream trucks or frietjes (pushcarts) for inexpensive, authentic Aruban finger food. Two worth the trip are El Rey Snack Truck near the Seaport Cinemas in Oranjestad, for freshly fried chicken, pork chops, and fries, and The Cellar Frietje in Oranjestad's Seaport Village Marketplace, for the best saté in town. Other island delicacies include the following:

BITTERBALLEN: steaming, bite-size meatballs. The long versions are served with mustard and called kroket. Locals wash down both varieties with beer.

FREKEDEL: a shredded fish dipped in egg and bread crumbs, rolled into balls, and deep fried.

FRIET OR BATATA: french fries—served in paper cones or Styrofoam cups—that can be topped with ketchup; mayo; curry, peanut, or hot sauce; onions; and more.

KESHI YENA: a baked concoction of Gouda cheese, spices, and meat or seafood in a rich brown sauce.

NASIBAL: a lump of seasoned rice in a crunchy coating.

PAN BATI: a pancake made of cornmeal, sugar, salt, and baking powder; eaten with meat, fish, or soup.

PASTECHI: deep-fried meat, cheese, potato, or seafood-filled turnovers, popular for breakfast. Smaller versions are called empanas.

RASPAO: a paper cup full of shaved ice that's drenched in tamarind, guava, or passion-fruit syrup.

ROTI: chicken, seafood, or vegetable curry in a tortilla-like wrap.

SATÉ: marinated chunks of chicken or pork on a bamboo skewer, grilled and served with spicy peanut sauce.

TOSTI: the ultimate grilled-cheese sandwich, often made with ham and pineapple or pepperoni.

Café

$$–$$$ **MOOMBA BEACH BAR & RESTAURANT.** Drop by anytime—this festive eatery serves breakfast, lunch, and dinner. By day, sit beneath the giant *palapa* (palm-covered enclosure) if you want to beat the heat, or plant yourself at a table in the sand if you haven't had enough sun. Every evening from 5 to 7 you can choose the special prix-fixe menu; for $19.95 you receive an appetizer, entrée, and dessert. As you wait for your food, enjoy a raspberry daiquiri while you watch the sunset. Once a month, the place is rollicking after hours with a full-moon dance party that lures all the island's night owls. *J. E. Irausquin Blvd. 230, Palm Beach, tel. 297/586–5365, www.moombabeach.com. AE, MC, V.*

Caribbean

$$–$$$$ **DRIFTWOOD.** Charming owner Francine Merryweather greets you at the door of this Aruban restaurant, which resembles a series of fishermen's huts. Her co-owner is likely out—personally reeling in your dinner. Order his catch prepared as you like (Aruban style—panfried with a fresh tomato, vegetable, and local herbs—is best) or another of the fine fish dishes. You can't go wrong with the white sangria punch; the maître d' may even let you take home the recipe. This restaurant participates in AGA's dine-around program. *Klipstraat 12, Oranjestad, tel. 297/583–2515. MC, V. Closed Tues.*

$$–$$$$ **GASPARITO RESTAURANT & ART GALLERY.** You'll find this
★   enchanting hideaway in a *cunucu* (country) house in Noord, not far from the hotels. Dine indoors, where works by local artists are showcased on softly lighted walls, or on the outdoor patio. Either way, the service is excellent. The Aruban specialties—pan bati, keshi yena, fish croquettes, conch stew—are feasts for the eye as well as the palate. The standout dish is the Gasparito chicken; the sauce was passed down from the owner's ancestors and features seven special ingredients, including brandy, white wine, and pineapple juice. (The rest, they say, are secret.) The restaurant

dining

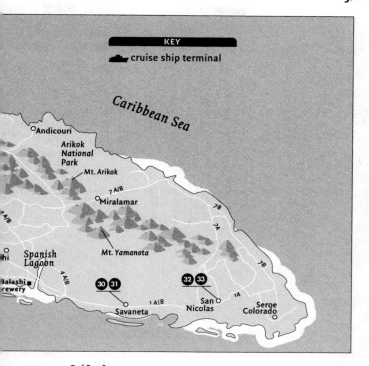

KEY

🚢 cruise ship terminal

Caribbean Sea

Andicouri

Arikok
National
Park

Mt. Arikok

7 A|B

Miralamar

7B

Mt. Yamanota

7A

Spanish
Lagoon

7B

hi

Balashi
rewery

4 A|B

30 31

32 33

1 A|B

Savaneta

San
Nicolas

1A

Seroe
Colorado

Some Like It Hot!

Arubans like their food spicy, and that's where the island's famous Madame Janette sauce comes in handy. It's made with chili peppers that are so hot they can burn your skin when they're broken open. Whether they're turned into pika, a relishlike mixture made with papaya, or sliced thin into vinegar and onions, these peppers are sure to set your mouth ablaze. Throw even a modest amount of Madame Janette sauce into a huge pot of soup and your taste buds will tingle. (Referring to the sauce's spicy nature, Aruban men often refer to an attractive woman as a "Madame Janette.")

To tame the flames, don't go for a glass of water, as capsaicin, the compound in peppers that produces the heat, isn't water soluble. Dairy products, sweet fruits, and starchy foods such as rice and bread are the best remedies.

participates in AGA's dine-around program. *Gasparito 3, Noord, tel. 297/586–7044. AE, D, MC, V. Closed Sun. No lunch.*

\$\$–\$\$\$\$ OLD CUNUCU HOUSE. Since the mid-1990s, executive chef Ligia Maria has delighted diners with delicious homemade meals, securing her reputation as one of Aruba's finest chefs. Try the keshi yena or the broiled Caribbean lobster tail served with thermidor cream sauce and topped with Parmesan cheese. For dessert, indulge in Spanish coffee with Tia Maria and brandy. Saturday night you can have all the fajitas you can eat. This restaurant participates in AGA's dine-around program. *Palm Beach 150, Noord, tel. 297/586–1666. AE, D, MC, V. No lunch.*

\$–\$\$\$ BRISAS DEL MAR. A meal at this friendly place overlooking the
★ sea is like dining in a private home. Old family recipes use such

indigenous ingredients as the aromatic *yerbiholé* leaf (with a minty basil flavor). Try the steamy fish soup, *keri keri* (shredded fish kissed with annatto), or some of the island's best pan bati. The catch of the day cooked Aruban-style (panfried and covered with creole sauce, or in garlic butter on request) has drawn a crowd for more than 20 years. Reserve early for sunset gazing on the breezy terrace. The restaurant is accessible by bus from most hotels. *Savaneta 222A, Savaneta, tel. 297/584–7718. AE, D, MC, V. Closed Mon.*

Contemporary

$$$–$$$$ **L'ESCALE.** You're missing out if you don't have at least one meal
★ at this elegant eatery, consistently ranked among the island's best. Sip a glass of wine as you gaze over bustling L. G. Smith Boulevard and watch the cruise ships depart. Start with the sautéed baby snails, then move on to Caribbean-style walnut-crusted snapper. For dessert try the rich chocolate soufflé. Sparkles and streamers adorn your table for special occasions, and the extensive cigar list can turn any night into a celebration. If time is short, opt for the speedy pretheater menu. *Renaissance Aruba Beach Resort & Casino, L. G. Smith Blvd. 82, Oranjestad, tel. 297/583–6000. Reservations essential. AE, D, MC, V. No lunch.*

$$–$$$$ **PASION.** Satisfy your passions for food, drink, and culture at this
★ seductive hot spot. Taste a few tapas before enjoying an entrée cooked up by the Colombian chef. The succulent fresh catch of the day is stewed with vegetables in foil, capturing the juices and aromas within. For dessert, the basil and passion-fruit mousse is a refreshingly creative option. The seating is intimate; large parties might choose to dine at the lovely communal table in the wooden wine cellar. The sommelier will help you choose the perfect wine from the extensive list to accompany your dinner. *Palm Beach Rd. 19A, Noord, tel. 297/586–4752, www.pasionbodega.com. Reservations essential. AE, D, MC, V. No lunch.*

$$–$$$ **RUMBA BAR & GRILL.** In the heart of Oranjestad, this lively bistro features an open kitchen where you can watch the chef prepare tasty international fare over a charcoal grill. The presentation is fanciful, with entrées forming towering shapes over beds of colorful vegetables and sauces. You can dine on the terrace and soak up the local color, or inside, where the crowd is always worth watching. This restaurant participates in AGA's dine-around program. *Havenstraat 4, Oranjestad, tel. 297/588–7900, www.rumba-aruba.com. AE, D, MC, V. Closed Sun. No lunch Sat.*

Continental

$$$–$$$$ **RUINAS DEL MAR.** Surrounded by lush landscaping and waterfalls, the "Ruins of the Sea" is the perfect spot for a romantic dinner—whether indoors or on the waterfront patio. Many of the exquisite dishes are given a Caribbean twist. The jerk-spice carpaccio with mustard sauce, peppers, and Parmesan cheese is tasty, as are the crab cakes with a habanero pepper hollandaise. The seafood mixed grill and veal chop in a fig marsala sauce are among the favored entrées. The Sunday champagne brunch buffet is a wonder. A 15% service charge is added to your check. *Hyatt Regency Aruba Beach Resort & Casino, J. E. Irausquin Blvd. 85, Palm Beach, tel. 297/586–1234. AE, D, DC, MC, V. No lunch.*

$$–$$$$ **★** **LE DÔME.** Belgian Peter Ballière and his partners imported 11,000 bricks from Antwerp to add European flair to this swank eatery. The service is polished, the decor is sumptuous, and a local harpist and guitarist add considerable ambience. The Belgian endive soup is delicious; the tournedos Rossini (prime-cut beef in a port sauce with a goose-liver mousse), downright decadent. If you can't decide, a seven-course set menu lets you sample a wide range of dishes. The wine list at this AGA VIP member includes more than 250 selections. Savor champagne with the prix-fixe Sunday brunch. *J. E. Irausquin Blvd. 224, Eagle Beach, tel. 297/587–1517, www.ledome-aruba.com. Reservations essential. AE, D, DC, MC, V. No lunch Sat.*

\$\$–\$\$\$ THE PROMENADE. A meal at this friendly yet elegant establishment is the perfect end to a day spent exploring San Nicolas and the island's eastern edge. The warm mood is accented by the yellow-and-green decor, which beckons you to sit back and relax. The catch of the day is prepared as you like it, and the seafood thermidor is a knockout. Portions are generous. The all-you-can-eat Sunday brunch (\$23 with champagne or a mimosa) is not only reasonably priced, but also festive, with live music. *Zeppenfeldstraat 15, San Nicolas, tel. 297/584–3131, www.promenadearuba.com. AE, D, DC, MC, V. Closed Mon.*

Cuban

\$\$–\$\$\$\$ CUBA'S COOKIN'. Locals (restaurateurs among them) agree that
★ the food here is "authentic ethnic." When you enter this old cunucu, head straight for the bar to order a *mojito*, a tasty mixture of light rum, sugar, mint, and soda. Afterward you can unwind in the art-filled dining room before digging into a truly Cuban dish such as *ropa vieja*, which, translated literally, means "old clothes." It's actually a sautéed skirt steak done to perfection. There's live music nightly at this restaurant, which participates in AGA's dine-around program. *Wilhelminastraat 27, Oranjestad, tel. 297/588–0627, www.cubascookin.com. AE, MC, V.*

Eclectic

\$\$\$–\$\$\$\$ PAPIAMENTO. Longtime restaurateurs Lenie and Eduardo Ellis
★ converted their 175-year-old manor into a bistro with an atmosphere that is elegant, intimate, and always romantic. You can feast in the dining room filled with antiques or outdoors on a terrace surrounding a pool. The chefs mix Continental and Caribbean cuisines to produce sumptuous seafood and meat dishes. You can't go wrong by sharing the "clay pot" seafood medley for two. *Washington 61, Noord, tel. 297/586–4544. Reservations essential. AE, D, MC, V. No lunch. Closed Mon.*

$$–$$$$ **MADAME JANETTE'S.** Dishes are presented with panache at this plucky restaurant, suitably named for a chili pepper. The menu reveals European standards alongside Caribbean favorites. The excitement starts with the bustle at the bar as you enter. It's a bit calmer once you're seated in the outdoor pebble garden, where tabletop candles cast a soft glow. Try the lamb or beef rotisseries with one of the special sauces; if you're in the mood for something lighter, there are tasty salads. For an overwhelming finish, top off your meal with a sundae that billows over the edges of a massive champagne glass. *Cunucu Abao 37, Cunucu Abao, tel. 297/587–0184, www.madamejanette.com. AE, MC, V. Closed Tues. No lunch.*

$$–$$$$ **CHARLIE'S RESTAURANT & BAR.** Charlie's has been a San Nicolas hangout for more than 50 years. The walls and ceiling are covered with license plates, hard hats, sombreros, life preservers, baseball pennants, intimate apparel—you name it. The draw here is the nonstop party atmosphere—somewhere between a frat house and a beach bar. Decent but somewhat overpriced specialties are tenderloin and "shrimps jumbo and dumbo" (dumb because they were caught). And don't leave before sampling Charlie's "honeymoon sauce" (so called because it's really hot). *Zeppenfeldstraat 56, San Nicolas, tel. 297/584–5086. AE, D, MC, V. Closed Sun.*

$$–$$$$ **VENTANAS DEL MAR.** Floor-to-ceiling windows provide an ample view across a golf course and beyond to rolling sand dunes and the sea off the island's western tip. Dining on the intimate terrace amid flickering candles inspires romance. Sandwiches, salads, conch fritters, nachos, and quesadillas fill the midday menu; at night the emphasis is on seafood and meat. Sea bass in orange sauce and crab-and-corn chowder are specialties. This restaurant is an AGA VIP member. *Tierra del Sol Golf Course, Malmokweg, tel. 297/586–7800. AE, D, DC, MC, V. Closed Mon. Apr.–Nov.*

$$–$$$ **BUCCANEER.** Imagine you're in a sunken ship where sharks, barracudas, and groupers swim past the portholes. That's what you'll find at Buccaneer, a restaurant with a fantastic 7,500-gallon saltwater aquarium. The chefs prepare surf-and-turf fare with European élan. Head early (around 5:45 PM) to this old stone building flanked by heavy black chains to snag a booth beside the aquarium and order the catch of the day, shrimp with Pernod, or smoked pork cutlets with sausage, sauerkraut, and potatoes. The restaurant participates in AGA's dine-around program. *Gasparito 11-C, Noord, tel. 297/586–6172. AE, D, MC, V. No lunch. Closed Sun.*

$$–$$$ CAPTAIN'S TABLE. The nautical surroundings might prompt you to try the cioppino, an Italian-style seafood stew, but the eclectic menu offers all sorts of other choices. Nightly piano music and a top-flight crew make for an all-around very pleasant dining experience. It's tough to choose from the extensive list of desserts, including no fewer than five options in the "death by chocolate" section. *La Cabana All Suite Beach Resort & Casino, J. E. Irausquin Blvd. 250, Eagle Beach, tel. 297/587–9000. AE, D, DC, MC, V.*

$$–$$$ LAGUNA. Louvered plantation-style doors frame the view at this colorful restaurant. You can dine inside in air-cooled comfort or outside on the terrace overlooking the lagoon. Enjoy the Indo-Caribbean stir-fry, the myriad seafood options, or something from the extensive sushi menu. Breakfast (either buffet or à la carte) is another possibility. *J. E. Irausquin Blvd. 81, Palm Beach, tel. 297/586–6555. AE, D, DC, MC, V. No lunch.*

$$–$$$ MARANDI. With a name that means "on the water" in Malaysian, this seaside restaurant is at once cozy and chic. Everything is seductive, from the tables tucked under a giant thatched roof by the water's edge to the dining room that's unencumbered by a ceiling. There are even couches set in a sandbox where you can enjoy a cocktail before your meal. Stellar entrées include the grouper fillet with a tapenade of sun-dried tomatoes or the pork tenderloin stuffed with prunes, coriander, and scallions. Reservations are essential for the special chef's table, where you dine right in the kitchen. *L. G. Smith Blvd. 1,*

Oranjestad, tel. 297/582–0157, www.marandiaruba.com. MC, V. No lunch. Closed Mon.

$$–$$$ QUÉ PASA? A sign on the wall at the bar welcomes you with a friendly WHAT'S HAPPENING? in several languages. Before grabbing a table, check out the local paintings on the walls. (You might even find one to bring home.) Specialties include lobster bisque, rib-eye steaks with shiitake mustard sauce, and raspberry pie. The amiable ambience on the terrace may prompt you to hang out after dinner and trade stories with the people at the next table. Wilhelminastraat 2, Oranjestad, tel. 297/583–4888, www.quepasaaruba.com. MC, V. No lunch.

¢–$$ COCO PLUM. Grab a pastechi (meat-, cheese-, or seafood-filled turnover) and go, or stick around to relax under thatch-roof huts and watch life unfold along Caya Betico Croes. Locals meet here for ham or tuna sandwiches, red snapper platters, and chicken wings. Slake your thirst with an all-natural fruit drink in flavors such as watermelon, lemon, papaya, tamarind, and passion fruit. At the counter, order loempias (egg rolls stuffed with vegetables, chicken, or shrimp) or empanas (stuffed pockets of cornmeal). Caya Betico Croes 100, Oranjestad, tel. 297/583–1176. AE, MC, V. No dinner. Closed Sun.

¢–$$ DELIFRANCE. If you're eager to skip the traditional hour-long hotel breakfast, DeliFrance offers the perfect solution—yummy, freshly baked baguettes and croissants. Try the All-American Breakfast Combo (toast, scrambled eggs, bacon, coffee, and fresh orange juice). Don't leave without tasting the Beukenhorst Koffie, a brand of Costa Rican java, and the poffertjes (miniature Dutch pancakes topped with melted butter and powdered sugar). For lunch there are salads, sandwiches, and, of course, pastries. The kids can play outside while you flip through American and European magazines. Certified Mega Mall, L. G. Smith Blvd. 150, Oranjestad, tel. 297/588–6006. AE, D, MC, V. No dinner.

Yo, Ho, Ho and a Cake of Rum

When Venancio Felipe Bareno came to Aruba from Spain more than a half century ago, little did he know that his family's rum cake recipe would make culinary history. Now the sweet little dessert is known around the world. His nephew, Bright Bakery owner Franklin Bareno, packages the pastry for local and international sales. The history of this island favorite is printed on the side of the box. Made with Aruban Palmeira rum, Natural Bridge Aruba's rum cake makes the perfect gift for folks back home. Available in two sizes, the vacuum-sealed cakes stay fresh for up to six months. The company is registered in the United States, so you can transport the cakes through customs.

French

$$$–$$$$ **★** **CHEZ MATHILDE.** Although this old house—Aruba's last 19th-century dwelling preserved in its original state—is not haunted, beware: the divine food, wine, and service may cast a spell on you. Ask to sit in the greenhouse atrium, with its whimsical Parisian-café-style decor. The outstanding French menu highlights the chef's deft touch with sauces, as in the ostrich fillet with five spices or coq au vin—braised hen cooked in red wine. The chocolate or Grand Marnier soufflé is intoxicating, as is the soothing piano music. The restaurant—run by descendants of the home's last inhabitant—is a VIP member of the AGA. *Havenstraat 23, Oranjestad, tel. 297/583–4968, www.chezmathilde.com. Reservations essential. AE, D, DC, MC, V. No lunch Sun.*

Italian

$$–$$$$ **HOSTARIA DA' VITTORIO.** Part of the fun at this family-oriented lunch and dinner spot is watching chef Vittorio Muscariello prepare authentic Italian regional specialties in the open kitchen. Rising above the decibel level of the crowd, the staff helps you choose wines from the extensive list and recommends portions of hot and cold antipasti, risottos, and pastas. Try the *branzino al sale* (sea bass baked in a hard salt shell). A 15% gratuity is automatically added to your bill at this VIP member of the AGA. As you leave, pick up some *limoncello* (lemon liqueur) at the gourmet shop. *L. G. Smith Blvd. 380, Palm Beach, tel. 297/586–3838. AE, D, MC, V.*

$$–$$$$ **TUSCANY.** The personalized service, excellent wine list, carefully prepared food, and soft piano music make for a special evening at this casually elegant restaurant. The *spannochie prima donna con capellini d'angelo* (sautéed shrimp with prosciutto, shallots, wild mushrooms, and artichokes in a light grappa cream sauce on angel hair pasta) is among the many delights. Don't despair if the extensive menu doesn't feature your particular fancy—the kitchen may be up for a challenge. *Aruba Marriott Resort & Stellaris Casino, L. G. Smith Blvd. 101, Palm Beach, tel. 297/586–9000. Reservations essential. AE, DC, MC, V. No lunch.*

Seafood

$$$–$$$$ **AQUA GRILL.** This hip restaurant is heaven on earth for seafood
★ lovers, who will find fresh fish galore and the island's largest raw bar. In fact, everything here is large in scale: from the wall of oversize windows to the big cherrywood tables with map-shaded lamps to the expansive glass wine rack to the boisterous din of the loftlike main dining room with a ceiling of exposed faux pipes. Seared tuna sashimi, oysters on the half shell, or steamer clams are good starters. Zesty entrées include cioppino—made here with lobster, shrimp, scallops, mussels, clams, and calamari in a light tomato sauce with red wine, saffron, fennel, and herbs—and

seared Chilean sea bass glazed with shallots, capers, and lemon. The restaurant is an AGA VIP member. *J. E. Irausquin Boulevard 374 Palm Beach, tel. 297/586–5900, www.aqua-grill.com. AE, DC, MC, V. No lunch.*

$$$–$$$$ **FLYING FISHBONE.** This restaurant is a little hard to find, but it's
★ worth the effort for a relaxing beachfront meal. The sultry Mediterranean decor transports you back to the days of *Casablanca* as soon as you walk through the door. Reserve a spot on the wooden deck that faces the ocean, or dig your toes into the sand at a table on the water's edge. Tuna, grouper, and other fresh catches are creatively prepared and artistically presented. *Savaneta 344, Savaneta, tel. 297/584–2506, www.flyingfishbone.com. AE, D, DC, MC, V. No lunch. Closed Sun.*

$$$ **WATERFRONT CRABHOUSE.** If you flew to Aruba on American Airlines, there might have been a 3,000-pound container of seafood in the belly of the plane. The restaurant receives a delivery of live Maine lobsters each day to stock its lobster tank—the largest in the Caribbean. Cajun-style lobster and shrimp is just one of the various preparations on the menu. A sirloin burger or crab-cake sandwich makes a tasty lunch. You can dine indoors or on the patio. The restaurant participates in AGA's dine-around program. *Seaport Village Marketplace, L. G. Smith Blvd. 9, Oranjestad, tel. 297/583–5858 or 297/583–6767. AE, D, DC, MC, V.*

Steak

$$$$ **AMAZONIA CHURRASCARIA.** The cozy surroundings and festive atmosphere will reel you in, but this Brazilian steak house offers much more. Charcoal-grilled meats are expertly prepared and charismatically carved right at your table, and the comprehensive salad bar includes items you didn't even know existed. Eat to your heart's content—it's all for a fixed price (excluding beverages and desserts). *J. E. Irausquin Blvd. 374, Palm Beach, tel. 297/586–4444, www.amazonia-aruba.com. AE, DC, MC, V. No lunch. Closed Mon.*

The Goods on Gouda

Each year Holland exports more than 250,000 tons of cheese to more than 100 countries, and Gouda (pronounced how-da) is one of the most popular. Gouda, named for the city where it's produced, travels well and gets harder, saltier, and more flavorful as it ages. There are six types of Gouda: young (at least 4 weeks old), semi-major (8 weeks old), major (4 months old), ultra-major (7 months old), old (10 months old), and vintage (more than a year old). When buying cheese in shops in Aruba, look for the control seal that confirms the name of the cheese, its country of origin, its fat content, and that it was officially inspected.

$$–$$$$ FRENCH STEAKHOUSE. You can hear someone say "ooh-la-la" whenever a sizzling steak is served. People come here from all over the island, which means the lines are often out the door. Classical music plays in the background as the friendly staff serves hearty meat entrées, fresh tuna or grouper, and even some vegetarian entrées. A five-course dinner includes a bottle of wine for a nice price. The eatery at the Manchebo Beach Resort participates in AGA's dine-around program. *J. E. Irausquin Blvd. 55, Eagle Beach, tel. 297/582–3444. AE, DC, MC, V. No lunch.*

Eating Well Is the Best Revenge

Eating out is a major part of every travel experience. It's a chance to explore flavors you don't find at home. And often the walking you do on vacation means that you can dig in without guilt.

START AT THE TOP By all means take in a really good restaurant or two while you're on the road. A trip is a time to kick back and savor the pleasures of the palate. Read up on the culinary scene before you leave home. Check out representative menus on the Web—some chefs have gone electronic. And ask friends who have just come back. Then reserve a table as far in advance as you can, remembering that the best establishments book up months in advance. Remember that some good restaurants require you to reconfirm the day before or the day of your meal. Then again, some really good places will call you, so make sure to leave a number where you can be reached.

ADVENTURES IN EATING A trip is the perfect opportunity to try food you can't get at home. So leave yourself open to try an ethnic food that's not represented where you live or to eat fruits and vegetables you've never heard of. One of them may become your next favorite food.

BEYOND GUIDEBOOKS You can rely on the restaurants you find in these pages. But also look for restaurants on your own. When you're ready for lunch, ask people you meet where they eat. Look for tiny holes-in-the-wall with a loyal following and the best burgers or crispiest pizza crust. Find out about local chains whose fame rests upon a single memorable dish. There's hardly a food-lover who doesn't relish the chance to share a favorite place. It's fun to come up with your own special find—and asking about food is a great way to start a conversation.

SAMPLE LOCAL FLAVORS Do check out the specialties. Is there a special brand of ice cream or a special dish that you simply must try?

HAVE A PICNIC Every so often eat al fresco. Grocery shopping gives you a whole different view of a place.

It was late in the day when the cruise ship docked. An agitated couple dashed into a jewelry shop and rushed to the gem counter, their shopping clock ticking. "Is anything wrong?" asked the clerk. "Well," said the woman, "our ship was delayed, and now we don't have time to buy all the things we wanted: earrings for my mother, a sarong for my sister, linens for our daughter, and a sculpture for our son." To accommodate the couple—and the 3,000 other passengers—the ship extended its stay until midnight and most shops in town remained open.

IN THIS CHAPTER

shopping

ARUBA'S SOUVENIR AND CRAFTS STORES ARE FULL of Dutch porcelains
and figurines, as befits the island's heritage. Dutch cheese is a good
buy (you're allowed to bring up to 10 pounds of hard cheese
through U.S. customs), as are hand-embroidered linens and any
products made from the native aloe vera plant—sunburn cream,
face masks, skin refreshers. Local arts and crafts run toward
wood carvings and earthenware emblazoned with ARUBA: ONE
HAPPY ISLAND and the like.

"Duty free" is a magical term. In fact, about 30% of the island's
annual cruise-ship visitors teem into the many duty-free stores
just steps from the terminal as soon as their ship docks. Most
North Americans, who find clothing to be less expensive back
home, buy perfume and jewelry; South Americans tend to shell
out lots of cash on a variety of brand-name merchandise.

Island merchants are honest and pleasant. Still, if you encounter
price markups, unsatisfactory service, or other shopping
obstacles, call the tourist office, which will in turn contact the
Aruba Merchants Association. A representative of the association
will speak with the merchant on your behalf, even if the store isn't
an association member.

HOW & WHEN

It's easy to spend money on Aruba. Most stores accept American
currency and Aruban florins (written as "Afl") as well as credit
cards and traveler's checks. Because there's no sales tax, the
price you see on the tag is what you pay. (Note that although

large stores in town and at hotels are duty free, in tiny shops and studios you may have to pay the ABB, or value-added tax, of 6.5%.) Don't try to bargain in stores, where it's considered rude to haggle. At flea markets and souvenir stands, however, you might be able to strike a deal.

At press time, two proposals that affect shopping hours were under consideration: one would extend store hours to 8 PM at least once each month; the other would force shops to close on Sunday. For now, stores are open Monday through Saturday 8:30 or 9 to 6. Some stores stay open through the lunch hour (noon–2), and many open when cruise ships are in port on Sundays and holidays. The later you shop in downtown Oranjestad, the easier it will be to find a place to park. Also, later hours mean slightly lower temperatures. In fact, the Aruba Merchants Association is one force behind the effort to have shops stay open later so that visitors who like to spend the day on the beach can shop in the cool of the evening.

AREAS & MALLS

Oranjestad's **CAYA G. F. BETICO CROES** is Aruba's chief shopping street, lined with several duty-free boutiques and jewelry stores noted for the aggressiveness of their vendors, especially on cruise-ship days. Most malls are in Oranjestad and are attractive gabled, pastel-hued re-creations of Dutch colonial architecture.

For late-night shopping, head to the **ALHAMBRA CASINO SHOPPING ARCADE** (L. G. Smith Blvd. 47, Manchebo Beach), open 5 PM–midnight. Souvenir shops, boutiques, and fast-food outlets fill the arcade, which is attached to the popular casino. Although small, the **AQUARIUS MALL** (Elleboogstraat 1, Oranjestad) has some upscale shops.

If you blink, you might miss the good finds at **DUTCH CROWN CENTER** (L. G. Smith Blvd. 150 [some shops face Havenstraat], Oranjestad), a tiny complex tucked between the major malls.

The **HOLLAND ARUBA MALL** (Havenstraat 6, Oranjestad) houses a collection of smart shops and eateries.

Stores at the **PORT OF CALL MARKETPLACE** (L. G. Smith Blvd. 17, Oranjestad) sell fine jewelry, perfumes, duty-free liquor, batiks, crystal, leather goods, and fashionable clothing. The **ROYAL PLAZA MALL** (L. G. Smith Blvd. 94, Oranjestad), across from the cruise-ship terminal, has cafés, a post office (open Monday–Friday 8–3:30), and such stores as Nautica, Benetton, Tommy Hilfiger, and Gandelman Jewelers. This is where you'll find the Cyber Café, where you can send e-mail and get your caffeine fix all in one stop.

Five minutes from the cruise-ship terminal, the **SEAPORT VILLAGE MALL** (L. G. Smith Blvd. 82, Oranjestad) is home to the Crystal Casino. More than 120 stores sell merchandise to meet every taste and budget. The pastel-hued **STRADA I AND STRADA II** (corner of Klipstraat and Rifstraat, Oranjestad) are shopping complexes in Dutch-style buildings.

SPECIALTY ITEMS

Cigars

You'll find fine cigars at **LA CASA DEL HABANO** (Royal Plaza Mall, L. G. Smith Blvd. 94, Oranjestad, tel. 297/583–8509). At the **CIGAR EMPORIUM** (Seaport Village Mall, L. G. Smith Blvd. 82, Oranjestad, tel. 297/582–5479), the Cubans come straight from the climate-controlled humidor. Choose from Cohiba, Montecristo, Romeo y Julieta, Partagas, and more. **SUPERIOR TOBACCO** (L. G. Smith Blvd. 120, Oranjestad, tel. 297/582–3220) is a good place to shop for stogies.

Clothes

★ If you're in the mood to splurge, **AGATHA BOUTIQUE** (Seaport Village Mall, L. G. Smith Blvd. 82, Oranjestad, tel. 297/583–7965) has some high-style outfits (some up to size 18), shoes,

Ronchi de Cuba's Aruban Style

"Shopping has recently become tremendously advanced on Aruba," says local fashion designer Ronchi de Cuba. "We're seeing higher-end fashion that's more reasonably priced, from companies like Fendi and Gucci, and the shopping area is still growing." He says the best time to get great buys at the high-end stores is in January, when the holidays are over and the racks are being cleared for the new season.

De Cuba became involved in fashion at age 17, thanks to a high school physical-education assignment for which he taught a dance class and presented a show that incorporated theater, choreography, and fashion. After attending college in Miami, de Cuba returned to his native Aruba to work at a modeling agency. Soon after, he opened his own agency to promote local entertainment and style.

The first Ronchi de Cuba design was a haute-couture number created for Miss Aruba 1999; he has since gone on to create ready-to-wear swimwear, menswear, womenswear, and junior lines. When he's not cutting clothes, the designer travels to New York, Miami, and Paris to peek into the shops and showrooms of major designers.

De Cuba clothes are constructed of fabrics suitable for a warm climate: crepe linens, silk georgettes, and shantungs for day; brocade, wool crepe, crepe de chine, and silk chiffon for evening. Inspired by such designers as John Galliano, Dolce & Gabbana, and Prada, his collections feature playful color schemes that incorporate dark solids, brights, and prints. He turns out a spring-summer collection and a holiday-cruise collection each year and held his first show in the United States in 2000. Always on the cutting edge of fashion, de Cuba is also known on the island for hosting the annual International Male Model contest, featuring dozens of contestants from the Caribbean, South and Central America, the United States, the United Arab Emirates, and Europe. After three days of water-sport competitions, beach parties, and bar hopping, the hopefuls compete at the event's grand finale at the Royal Cabana Casino, showing off swimwear by—you guessed it—de Cuba himself. Look for his label at stores in the Seaport Village Marketplace and the Royal Plaza Mall or at his own shop—Revolution—in Oranjestad.

and bags by New York fashion designer Agatha Brown. Sample at least one of her two signature fragrances, derived from floral and citrus scents.

People come to **CAPERUCITA RAJA** (Wilhelminastraat 17, Oranjestad, tel. 297/583–6166) for designer baby, children's, and junior clothes, as well as a wide selection of shoes. Outfits that cost $21 here sell for more than three times that amount at Saks Fifth Avenue. Forget to pack your intimates? **COLOMBIA MODA** (Wilhelminastraat 19, Oranjestad, tel. 297/582–3460) will help complete your wardrobe with lingerie made of high-quality microfiber fabrics. **CONFETTI** (Seaport Village Mall, L. G. Smith Blvd. 82, Oranjestad, tel. 297/583–8614) has the hottest European and American swimsuits, cover-ups, and other beach essentials.

★ **DEL SOL** (Royal Plaza Mall, L. G. Smith Blvd. 94, Oranjestad, tel. 297/583–8448) is the place to buy beach accessories such as sun visors, and shirts and shorts that change colors in the sun. **EXTREME SPORTS** (Royal Plaza Mall, L. G. Smith Blvd. 94, Oranjestad, tel. 297/583–8458) sells everything sportsaholics could ever need. Invest in a set of in-line skates or a boogie board, or pick up a backpack, bathing suit, or pair of reef walkers in funky shades. A venerated name in Aruba, **J. L. PENHA & SONS** (Caya G. F. Betico Croes 11/13, Oranjestad, tel. 297/582–4160 or 297/582–4161) sells high-end perfumes and cosmetics. It stocks such brands as Boucheron, Cartier, Dior, and Givenchy.

At **MANGO** (Main St. 9, Oranjestad, tel. 297/582–9700)—part of an international chain—you'll find fashions from as far away as Spain. **MODA ACTUAL** (Caya G. F. Betico Croes 49, Oranjestad, tel. 297/583–1202) rotates its reasonably priced, high-quality merchandise about every two months. Popular items include preshrunk cotton tank tops and T-shirts for men and women. If the Aruban sun doesn't make your life sizzle, the sexy lingerie at **SECRETS OF ARUBA** (Seaport Village Mall, L. G. Smith Blvd. 82, Oranjestad, tel. 297/583–0897) just might. The store also sells oils and lotions that aren't used for getting a tan. As the many repeat customers will tell you, **SUN + SAND** (Dutch Crown Center, L. G. Smith Blvd. 150, Oranjestad, tel. 297/583–8812) is the place for T-shirts, sweatshirts, polo shirts, and cover-ups.

For innovative activewear, check out **TOMMY HILFIGER** (Royal Plaza Mall, L. G. Smith Blvd. 94, Oranjestad, tel. 297/583–8548). Be sure to visit the Tommy Jeans store as well. Menswear reigns supreme at **LA VENEZOLANA** (Steenweg 12, Oranjestad, tel. 297/582–1444). You'll find blazers and suits as well as jeans, belts, and shoes. Look for such names as Givenchy, Lee Jeans, and Van Heusen.

★ **WULFSEN & WULFSEN** (Caya G. F. Betico Croes 52, Oranjestad, tel. 297/582–3823) has been one of the most highly regarded clothing stores in Aruba and the Netherlands Antilles for 30 years. It carries elegant suits for men and linen cocktail dresses for women, and it's also a great place to buy bathing suits and Bermuda shorts.

Duty-Free Goods

For perfumes, cosmetics, men's and women's clothing, and leather goods (including Bally shoes), stop in at **ARUBA TRADING COMPANY** (Caya G. F. Betico Croes 12, Oranjestad, tel. 297/582–2602), which has been in business for nearly 75 years.

★ **LITTLE SWITZERLAND** (Caya G. F. Betico Croes 14, Oranjestad, tel. 297/582–1192; Royal Plaza Mall, L. G. Smith Blvd. 94, Oranjestad, tel. 297/583–4057), the St. Thomas–based giant, is the place to go for china, crystal, and fine tableware. You'll also find good buys on Omega and Rado watches, Swarovski and Baccarat crystal, and Lladro figurines.

At **WEITNAUER** (Caya G. F. Betico Croes 29, Oranjestad, tel. 297/582–2790) you'll find specialty Lenox items as well as a wide range of fragrances.

Food

The clean, orderly **KONG HING SUPERMARKET** (L. G. Smith Blvd. 152, Bushiri, tel. 297/582–5545) stocks all the comforts of home—from fresh cuts of meat to prepackaged salads to Lean Cuisine dinners. The liquor section offers everything from exotic liqueurs to familiar beers. There's also a pharmacy with name-brand items such as Goody hair supplies and Bausch & Lomb eye-care products. The market, which is open Monday to Saturday 8–8 and Sunday 9–1, accepts Discover, MasterCard, and Visa for purchases of $10 or more. There's an ATM on the premises.

The family-owned and -operated **LING & SONS SUPERMARKET** (Italiestraat 26, Eagle Beach, tel. 297/583–2370, www.visitaruba.com/ling&sons) is one of the island's top grocers. In addition to a wide variety of foods, there's a bakery, a deli, a butcher shop, and a well-stocked "liquortique." If you e-mail ahead, the store can have a package of essential foodstuffs delivered to your hotel room in time for your arrival. The market is open Monday to Saturday 8–8 and Sunday 9–1. Before the December holidays, the store sometimes stays open an hour later on weekdays.

Gifts & Souvenirs

★ **ART & TRADITION HANDICRAFTS** (Caya G. F. Betico Croes 30, Oranjestad, tel. 297/583–6534; Royal Plaza Mall, L. G. Smith Blvd. 94, Oranjestad, tel. 297/582–7862) sells intriguing souvenirs. Buds from the *mopa mopa* tree are boiled to form a resin colored by vegetable dyes. Artists then stretch the resin by hand and mouth. Tiny pieces are cut and layered to form intricate designs—truly unusual gifts.

The **ARTISTIC BOUTIQUE** (Caya G. F. Betico Croes 25, Oranjestad, tel. 297/582–3142; Wyndham Aruba Beach Resort & Casino, J. E. Irausquin Blvd. 77, tel. 297/586–4466 Ext. 3508; Seaport Village Mall, L. G. Smith Blvd. 82, Oranjestad, tel. 297/583–2567; Holiday

Inn Sunspree Aruba Beach Resort & Casino, J. E. Irausquin Blvd. 230, tel. 297/583–3383) has been in business for more than 30 years. It's known for its Giuseppe Armani figurines from Italy, usually sold at a 20% discount; Aruban hand-embroidered linens; gold and silver jewelry; and porcelain and pottery from Spain.

EL BOHIO (Holiday Inn Sunspree Aruba Beach Resort & Casino, Port of Call Marketplace, L. G. Smith Blvd. 17, Oranjestad, tel. 297/582–9178) will charm you with its wooden-hut displays holding Arawak-style pottery, Dutch shoes, and wind chimes. You'll also find classic leather handbags. **CREATIVE HANDS** (Socotorolaan 5, Oranjestad, tel. 297/583–5665) sells porcelain and ceramic miniatures of *cunucu* (country) houses and divi-divi trees, but the store's real draw is its exquisite Japanese dolls. For pottery lovers, **KWA KWA** (Port of Call Marketplace, L. G. Smith Blvd. 17, Oranjestad, tel. 297/583–9471) is a paradise. There are wind chimes, pottery, and knickknacks galore—all made of ceramic, of course. Other items include embroidered bags.

While you wait 30 minutes for your film to be developed at **NEW FACE PHOTO** (Dutch Crown Center, Havenstraat 27, Oranjestad, tel. 297/582–9510), you can shop for gifts. At **VIBES** (Royal Plaza Mall, L. G. Smith Blvd. 93, Oranjestad, tel. 297/583–7949) treat yourself to a Monte Crisco or Cohiba cigar, and pick up souvenirs such as postcards, picture frames, and T-shirts. Clothes from Aruba and Indonesia, hand-painted mobiles, and bamboo wind chimes are among the goodies at **TROPICAL WAVE** (Port of Call Marketplace, L. G. Smith Blvd. 17, Oranjestad, tel. 297/582–1905).

Housewares

Locals swear by **DECOR HOME FASHIONS** (Steenweg 14, Oranjestad, tel. 297/582–6620), which sells sheets, towels, place mats, and other linens imported from Italy, Germany, Holland, Portugal, and the United States.

Jewelry

Filling 6,000 square feet of space, **BOOLCHAND'S** (Seaport Village Mall, L. G. Smith Blvd. 82, Oranjestad, tel. 297/583–0147) sells jewelry and watches. It also stocks leather goods, cameras, and electronics. If green fire is your passion, **COLOMBIAN EMERALDS** (Seaport Village Mall, L. G. Smith Blvd. 82, Oranjestad, tel. 297/583–6238) has a dazzling array. There are also fine watches by Raymond Weil, Baume & Mercier, Jaeger-Le Coultre, Ebel, Seiko, Citizen, and Tissot. For all that glitters, head to **DIAMONDS INTERNATIONAL** (Port of Call Marketplace, L. G. Smith Blvd. 17, Oranjestad, tel. 800/515–3935).**GANDELMAN JEWELERS** (Royal Plaza Mall, L. G. Smith Blvd. 94, Oranjestad, tel. 297/583–4433) sells Gucci and Rolex watches at reasonable prices. The store also has gold bracelets and a full line of Lladro figurines. Find one-of-a-kind silver
★ pieces at **GRACE SILVER & BEYOND** (Seaport Marketplace 13, L. G. Smith Blvd. 9, Oranjestad, tel. 297/588–6262). **KENRO JEWELERS** (Seaport Village Mall, L. G. Smith Blvd. 82, Oranjestad, tel. 297/583–4847 or 297/583–3171) has two stores in the same mall, attesting to the popularity of its stock of bracelets and necklaces from Ramon Leopard; jewelry by Arando, Micheletto, and Blumei; and various brands of watches. There are also six other locations, including some in the major hotels.

Precious pearls add lustre to many of the pretty items at **PEARL GEMS FINE JEWELRY** (L. G. Smith Blvd. 90-92, Oranjestad, tel. 297/588–4927).

Leather Goods

ALIVIO (Steenweg 12-1, Oranjestad, no phone) has shoes for men, women, and children. Whether you're walking around town by day or dressing up for dinner by night, you'll find something suitable in this shop in Oranjestad. Look for Birkenstock from Germany, Piedro and Wolky from Holland, and Mephisto from France.

If you get lucky, you'll catch one of the year's big sales (one is held the first week in December, the other the first week in February) at **GUCCI** (Seaport Village Mall, L. G. Smith Blvd. 82, Oranjestad, tel. 297/583–3952), when prices are slashed on handbags, luggage, wallets, shoes, watches, belts, and ties. **FERRAGAMO** (Emmastraat 1, Oranjestad, tel. 297/582–8218) has a popular boutique behind Royal Plaza Mall.

Beyond T-Shirts and Key Chains

You can't go wrong with baseball caps, refrigerator magnets, beer mugs, sweatshirts, T-shirts, key chains, and other local logo merchandise. You won't go broke buying these items, either.

BUDGET FOR A MAJOR PURCHASE If souvenirs are all about keeping the memories alive in the long haul, plan ahead to shop for something really special—a work of art, a rug or something else hand-crafted, or a major accessory for your home. One major purchase will stay with you far longer than a dozen tourist trinkets, and you'll have all the wonderful memories associated with shopping for it besides.

ADD TO YOUR COLLECTION Whether antiques, used books, salt and pepper shakers, or ceramic frogs are your thing, start looking in the first day or two. Chances are you'll want to scout around and then go back to some of the first shops you visited before you hand over your credit card.

GET GUARANTEES IN WRITING Is the vendor making promises? Ask him to put them in writing.

ANTICIPATE A SHOPPING SPREE If you think you might buy breakables, include a length of bubble wrap. Pack a large tote bag in your suitcase in case you need extra space. Don't fill your suitcase to bursting before you leave home. Or include some old clothing that you can leave behind to make room for new acquisitions.

KNOW BEFORE YOU GO Study prices at home on items you might consider buying while you're away. Otherwise you won't recognize a bargain when you see one.

PLASTIC, PLEASE Especially if your purchase is pricey and you're looking for authenticity, it's always smart to pay with a credit card. If a problem arises later on and the merchant can't or won't resolve it, the credit-card company may help you out.

Oblivious to the casino's din, a handful of blackjack players are on the edge of their seats. Each has split his or her cards, and there's a lot of money at stake. The dealer's hand totals 16. One player wipes the sweat from his brow; another takes a long drag on her cigarette and slowly exhales. A group of onlookers whisper their predictions. With a flourish, the dealer pulls his final card—a queen! The players shout for joy.

In This Chapter

casinos

THERE WAS A TIME WHEN WOMEN DRESSED in evening gowns and men donned suits for a chic, glamorous night in Aruba's casinos. In the mid-'80s, however, the Alhambra Casino opened, touting its philosophy of "barefoot elegance." Suddenly shorts and T-shirts became acceptable attire. The relaxed dress code made gaming seem an affordable pastime rather than a luxury.

Aruba's casinos now attract high rollers, low-stakes bettors, and nongamblers alike. Games include slot machines, blackjack (both beloved by North Americans), baccarat (preferred by South Americans), craps, roulette—even betting on sports events. Theaters, restaurants, bars, and cigar shops have added another dimension to the casinos. Now you can go out for dinner, take in a show, sip after-dinner drinks, and play blackjack all under one roof. In between games, you can get to know other patrons and swap tips and tales. The many local entertainers who rotate among the casinos add to the excitement.

THE CASINOS

Except for the free-standing Alhambra, most casinos are found in hotels; all are along Palm Beach or Eagle Beach or in downtown Oranjestad. Although the minimum age to enter is 18, some venues are relaxed about this rule. By day, "barefoot elegance" is the norm in all casinos, although many establishments have a shirt-and-shoes requirement. Evening dress is expected to be more polished, though still casual. In high season, the casinos are open from just before noon to the wee hours; in low season

(May to November), they may not start dealing until late afternoon.

If you plan to play large sums of money, check in with the casino upon arrival so that you'll be rewarded for your business. Most hotels offer gambling goodies—complimentary meals at local restaurants, chauffeured tours, and, in the cases of big winners, high-roller suites—for patrons spending a lot of cash. Even small-scale gamblers may be entitled to coupons for meals and discounted rooms.

★ **ALHAMBRA CASINO.** Here, amid the Spanish-style arches and leaded glass, a "Moorish slave" named Roger gives every gambler a hearty handshake upon entering. The atmosphere is casual, and with $5 tables, no one need feel intimidated. Try your luck at blackjack, Caribbean stud poker, three-card poker, roulette, craps, or one of the 300 slot machines that accept American nickels, quarters, and dollars. Head to one of the novelty touch-screen machines, each of which has a variety of games. There's also bingo every Saturday, Monday, and Thursday beginning at 1 PM. If you fill your card, you can collect the grand prize of a few hundred dollars—not bad for a $5 investment. Be sure to sign up for the Alhambra Advantage Card, which gives you a point for each dollar you spend—even if you lose at the tables, you can still go home with prizes. Of course, winners can spend their earnings immediately at the many on-site shops. The casino is owned by the Divi Divi resorts, and golf carts run to and from nearby hotels every 15 minutes or so. The slots here open daily at 10 AM; gaming tables operate from 6 PM until 4 AM. *L. G. Smith Blvd. 47, Oranjestad, tel. 297/583–5000 Ext. 480 or 482.*

ALLEGRO CASINO. Famous movie stars gaze down at you from a 30-foot mural as you take your chance at one of 245 slots or at dozens of blackjack, roulette, poker, craps, baccarat, and Caribbean stud poker tables. The casino at the Occidental Allegro Resort opens daily at noon for slots and at 5 PM for all other games. The entire gaming floor joins in the free full-card bingo game held nightly at 10:30. Anyone who scores a full card within the first 50 calls wins a clean grand; everyone who shows a full card after that walks away with $100. Friday at 8 PM sees a slot tournament, and look for double jackpots daily from 3 to 5 PM. You can hang around until 4 AM. J. E. Irausquin Blvd. 83, Palm Beach, tel. 297/586–9039, www.allegroresorts.com.

CARNAVAL CASINO. Real musical instruments decorate the walls of this small, homey establishment in the Aruba Grand Beach Resort. The clientele is flecked with lawyers and accountants fresh from the States. Like you, they've come to play blackjack, roulette, craps, poker, and slots. Look for such theme nights as Lucky Joker Night, when the recipient of a secret joker stashed in a blackjack deck wins a cash prize. The casino opens at 10 AM for slots and 6 PM for the tables. The fun doesn't end until 2 AM. J. E. Irausquin Blvd. 79, Palm Beach, tel. 297/586–3900 Ext. 149, www.arubagrand.com.

CASABLANCA CASINO. Smart money is on the Wyndham Aruba Beach Resort's quietly elegant casino, which has a Humphrey Bogart theme and a tropical color scheme. Spend some time at the blackjack, roulette, craps, stud poker, and baccarat tables, or the slot machines. Seek out the unique Feature Frenzy machines, which reportedly pay out $6,000 jackpots daily. If gambling isn't your style, visit the Sirocco Lounge for exotic cocktails and live jazz most nights at 9. Or you can take in the Aruba Carnival Havana Tropical shows. The casino is open daily from noon to 4 AM. J. E. Irausquin Blvd. 77, Palm Beach, tel. 297/586–4466, www.wyndham.com.

CASINO AT THE RADISSON ARUBA RESORT. Although it measures 16,000 square feet, you may have a hard time finding this casino. Descend the stairs at the corner of the resort's lobby, following the sounds of the piano player's tunes. The nightly action here includes Las Vegas–style blackjack, roulette, craps, and slot machines. Overhead, thousands of lights simulate shooting stars that seem destined to carry out your wishes for riches. A host of shops and restaurants let you chip away at your newfound wealth. The slots here open daily at noon, and the table action begins at 6 PM. Everything shuts down at 4 AM. J. E. Irausquin Blvd. 81, Palm Beach, tel. 297/586–4045, www.radisson.com.

★ **COPACABANA CASINO.** Ablaze with neon, the Hyatt Regency Aruba Beach Resort's ultramodern casino is an enormous complex with a Carnival-in-Rio theme. The most popular games here are slots, blackjack, craps, and baccarat. Slots and some other games are available at noon, the dice start rolling at 6 PM, and all other pursuits are open by 8 PM. From 9 PM to 2 AM, there's live music at the stage near the bar. You'll find it hard to steal away from the pulsating mix of Latin and American tunes. Don't forget to register for free dinners and brunches and hotel discounts at the hostess station. The casino is open until 4 AM. J. E. Irausquin Blvd. 85, Palm Beach, tel. 297/586–1234, www.hyatt.com.

CRYSTAL CASINO. Adorned with Austrian crystal chandeliers and gold-leaf columns, the Renaissance Aruba Beach Resort Marina Tower's glittering casino evokes Monaco's grand establishments—hence, the international clientele. The Salon Privé offers serious gamblers a private room for baccarat, roulette, and high-stakes blackjack. This casino is popular among cruise-ship passengers, who stroll over from the port to watch and play in slot tournaments and bet on sporting events. The Crystal Lounge, which overlooks the betting floor, serves up live music along with the cocktails, and the Crystal Theater's shows—*Let's Go Latin* and *Aruba Panorama*—are big hits on the island. L. G. Smith Blvd. 82, Oranjestad, tel. 297/583–6000, www.arubarenaissance.com.

EXCELSIOR CASINO. The Holiday Inn SunSpree Aruba Beach Resort's casino—the birthplace of Caribbean stud poker—has blackjack, craps, and roulette tables, plenty of slot machines, and a bar featuring live entertainment. There's also a poker room for Texas hold 'em, seven-card stud, and Caribbean stud. It's the only casino on Palm Beach with an ATM adjacent to the cashier.

Good Luck Charms

Arubans take myths and superstitions very seriously. They flinch if a black butterfly flits into their home, because this symbolizes death. They gasp if a child crawls under their legs, because it's a sign that the baby won't grow anymore. And on New Year's Eve, they toss the first sips of whiskey, rum, or champagne from the first bottle that's opened in the New Year out the door of their house to show respect to those who have died and to wish luck on others. It's no surprise, then, that good luck charms are part of Aruba's casino culture as well.

The island's most common good luck charm is the djucu (pronounced joo-koo), a brown-and-black stone that comes from the sea and becomes hot when rubbed. They're sold at the convenience store near the Natural Bridge, and many people have them put in gold settings—with their initials engraved in the metal—and wear them around their necks on a chain with other charms such as an anchor or a cross. Another item that's thought to bring good luck is a small bag of sand. Women wear them tucked discreetly into their bras; one woman who visited Aruba every year always carried a few cloves of garlic in her bag. On a recent visit, she removed the garlic, placed it on a slot machine, and won $1,000 instantly. All the more reason to save the scraps from your salad plate when you leave dinner.

Afternoon bingo overtakes the main floor every weekday at 3:30 PM. The casino is open daily from 8 AM to 4 AM; slots begin spinning at 9 AM and tables open at 12:30 PM. J. E. Irausquin Blvd. 230, Palm Beach, tel. 297/586–3600, www.holidayinn-aruba.com.

ROYAL CABANA CASINO. Reputedly the largest casino in the Caribbean, Royal Cabana has a sleek interior that holds 372 slot machines. If you like bingo, the casino offers the highest-stakes games around Monday to Saturday at 1 PM and 3:30 PM. The Tropicana Showroom is known for the energy of such hit shows as Don't Tell Mama and La Cage aux Folles. The slots here open daily at 11 AM, the tables at 4 PM. The casino, next door to the La Cabana All Suite Beach Resort, closes at 4 AM. J. E. Irausquin Blvd. 250, Eagle Beach, tel. 297/587–4665, www.lacabana.com.

SEAPORT CASINO. The gambling is low key at this waterside establishment adjacent to the Renaissance Aruba Beach Resort's Beach Tower, the Seaport Marketplace, and the Seaport Conference Center. More than 200 slot machines are in daily operation from 10 AM to 4 AM, and tables are open from 4 PM to 4 AM. From here, you can see the boats on the ocean and enjoy not only the games you'd find at other casinos but also shops, restaurants, bars, and movie theaters. Stop by on Tuesday, Thursday, or Sunday for the casino's popular bingo tournaments. L. G. Smith Blvd. 9, Oranjestad, tel. 297/583–5027 Ext. 4212.

★ **STELLARIS CASINO.** The Aruba Marriott Resort's casino has mirrors on the ceilings that reflect the glamorous chandeliers. Start at the slots at noon or the tables at 4 PM and play until 4 AM if you're on a roll. Take your pick of craps, roulette, Caribbean stud poker, minibaccarat, and superbuck (like blackjack with suits). Every night except Sunday there's a performance by musician Cesar Olarta that may boost your luck. Check in with the casino when you arrive at the hotel and you'll get a membership card. If you play high enough stakes at the tables, you can win free meals and other prizes. If not, you'll at least get a postcard in the mail offering a special rate on future stays. The hotel offers a 30% discount to those who play at least four hours each day. *L. G. Smith Blvd. 101, Palm Beach, tel. 297/586–9000, www.marriott.com.*

THE GAMES

For a short-form handbook on the rules, the odds, and the strategies for the most popular casino games—or for help deciding on the kind of action that suits your style—read on.

The first part of any casino strategy is to risk the most money on wagers that present the lowest edge for the house. Blackjack, craps, video poker, and baccarat are the most advantageous to the bettor. The two types of bets at baccarat have a house advantage of a little more than 1%. The basic line bets at craps, if backed up with full odds, can be as low as 0.5%. Blackjack and video poker can not only put you even with the house (a true 50-50 proposition) but give you a slight long-term advantage.

How can a casino provide you with a 50-50 or even a positive expectation at some of its games? First, because a vast number of suckers make bad bets (those with a house advantage of 5%–35%, such as roulette, keno, and slots). Second, because the casino knows that very few people are aware of the opportunities to beat the odds. Third, because it takes skill to exploit these opportunities. However, a mere hour or two spent learning strategies for the beatable games will put you ahead of most visitors, who give the gambling industry an average 12%–15% profit margin.

BACCARAT

The most "glamorous" game in the casino, baccarat is a version of *chemin de fer*, which is popular in European gambling halls. It's a favorite with high rollers because thousands of dollars are often staked on one hand. The Italian word *baccara* means "zero." This refers to the point value of 10s and picture cards.

The game is run by four pit personnel. Two dealers sit side by side at the middle of the table. They handle the winning and losing bets and keep track of each player's "commission" (explained below). The caller stands in the middle of the other side of the table and dictates the action. The "ladderman" supervises the game and acts as final judge if any disputes arise.

How to Play

Baccarat is played with eight decks of cards dealt from a large "shoe" (or cardholder). Each player is offered a turn at handling the shoe and dealing the cards. Two two-card hands are dealt: the "player" and the "bank" hands. The player who deals the cards is called the banker, although the house banks both hands. The players bet on which hand—player or banker—will come closest to adding up to 9 (a "natural"). Ace through 9 retain face value, and 10s and picture cards are worth zero. If you have a hand adding up to more than 10, the number 10 is subtracted from the total. For example, if one hand contains a 10 and a 4, the hand adds up to 4. If the other holds an ace and a 6, it adds up to 7. If a hand has a 7 and a 9, it adds up to 6.

Depending on the two hands, the caller either declares a winner and loser (if either hand actually adds up to 8 or 9) or calls for another card for the player hand (if it totals 1, 2, 3, 4, 5, or 10). The bank hand then either stands pat or draws a card, determined by a complex series of rules depending on what the player's total is and dictated by the caller. When one or the other hand is declared a winner, the dealers go into action to pay off the winning wagers, collect the losing wagers, and add up the commission (usually 5%) that the house collects on the bank hand. Both bets have a house advantage of slightly more than 1%.

The player-dealer (or banker) holds the shoe as long as the bank hand wins. When the player hand wins, the shoe moves counterclockwise around the table. Players can refuse the shoe and pass it to the next player. Because the caller dictates the action, player responsibilities are minimal. It's not necessary to know the card-drawing rules, even if you're the banker.

Baccarat Strategy

To bet you only have to place your money in the bank, player, or tie box on the layout, which appears directly in front of where you sit. If you're betting that the bank hand will win, you put your chips in the bank box; bets for the player hand go in the player box. (Only real suckers bet on the tie.) Most players bet on the bank hand when they deal, since they "represent" the bank and to do otherwise would seem as if they were betting "against" themselves. This isn't really true, but it seems that way. Playing baccarat is a simple matter of guessing whether the player or banker hand will come closest to 9 and deciding how much to bet on the outcome.

BLACKJACK

How to Play

You play blackjack against a dealer, and whichever of you comes closest to a card total of 21 wins. Number cards are worth their face value, picture cards are worth 10, and aces are worth either 1 or 11. (Hands with aces are known as "soft" hands. Always count the ace first as an 11. If you also have a 10, your total will be 21, not 11.) If the dealer has a 17 and you have a 16, you lose. If you have an 18 against a dealer's 17, you win (even money). If both you and the dealer have a 17, it's a tie (or "push") and no money changes hands. If you go over a total of 21 (or "bust"), you lose, even if the dealer also busts later in the hand. If your first two cards add up to 21 (a "natural"), you're paid 3 to 2. However, if the dealer also has a natural, it's a push. A natural beats a total of 21 achieved with more than two cards.

You're dealt two cards, either facedown or faceup, depending on the custom of the casino. The dealer also gives herself two cards, one facedown and one faceup (except in double-exposure blackjack, where both the dealer's cards are visible). Depending on your first two cards and the dealer's up card, you can **stand,** or refuse to take another card. You can **hit,** or take as many cards as you need until you stand or bust. You can **double down,** or double your bet and take one card. You can **split** a like pair; if you're dealt two 8s, for example, you can double your bet and play the 8s as if they're two hands. You can **buy insurance** if the dealer is showing an ace. Here you're wagering half your initial bet that the dealer *does* have a natural. If so, you lose your initial bet but are paid 2 to 1 on the insurance (which means the whole thing is a push). You can **surrender** half your initial bet if you're holding a bad hand (known as a "stiff") such as a 15 or 16 against a high-up card such as a 9 or 10.

Blackjack Strategy

Many people devote a great deal of time to learning complicated statistical schemes. However, if you don't have the time, energy, or inclination to get that seriously involved, the following basic strategies should allow you to play the game with a modicum of skill and a paucity of humiliation:

When your hand is a stiff (a total of 12, 13, 14, 15, or 16) and the dealer shows a 2, 3, 4, 5, or 6, always stand.

When your hand is a stiff and the dealer shows a 7, 8, 9, 10, or ace, always hit.

When you hold 17, 18, 19, or 20, always stand.

When you hold a 10 or 11 and the dealer shows a 2, 3, 4, 5, 6, 7, 8, or 9, always double down.

When you hold a pair of aces or a pair of 8s, always split.

Never buy insurance.

CRAPS

Craps is a dice game played at a large rectangular table with rounded corners. Up to 12 players can stand around the table. The layout is mounted at the bottom of a surrounding rail, which prevents the dice from being thrown off the table and provides an opposite wall against which to bounce the dice. It can require up to four pit personnel to run an action-packed, fast-paced game of craps. Two dealers handle the bets made on either side of the layout. A "stickman" wields the long wooden stick, curved at one end, which is used to move the dice around the table. The stickman also calls the number that's rolled and books the proposition bets made in the middle of the layout. The "boxman" sits between the two dealers, overseeing the game and settling any disputes.

How to Play

Stand at the table wherever you can find an open space. You can start betting casino chips immediately, but you have to wait your turn to be the shooter. The dice are passed clockwise around the table (the stickman will give you the dice at the appropriate time). It's important, when you're the shooter, to roll the dice hard enough so they bounce off the end wall of the table. This shows that you're not trying to control the dice with a "soft roll."

Craps Strategy

Playing craps is fairly straightforward; it's the betting that's complicated. The basic concepts are as follows: If the first time the shooter rolls the dice he or she turns up a 7 or 11, that's called a "natural"—an automatic win. If a 2, 3, or 12 comes up on the first throw (called the "come-out roll"), that's termed "craps"—an automatic lose. Each of the numbers 4, 5, 6, 8, 9, or 10 on a first roll is known as a "point": the shooter keeps rolling the dice until the point comes up again. If a 7 turns up before the point does, that's another loser. When either the point or a losing 7 is rolled, this is known as a "decision," which happens on average every 3.3 rolls.

But "winning" and "losing" rolls of the dice are entirely relative in this game, because there are two ways you can bet at craps: "for" the shooter or "against" the shooter. Betting for means that the shooter will "make his point" (win). Betting against means that the shooter will "seven out" (lose). Either way, you're actually betting against the house, which books all wagers. If you're betting "for" on the come-out, you place your chips on the layout's "pass line." If a 7 or 11 is rolled, you win even money. If a 2, 3, or 12 (craps) is rolled, you lose your bet. If you're betting "against" on the come-out, you place your chips in the "don't pass bar." A 7 or 11 loses; a 2, 3, or 12 wins. A shooter can bet for or against himself, or against other players.

There are also roughly two dozen wagers you can make on any single specific roll of the dice. Craps strategy books can give you the details on come/don't come, odds, place, buy, big six, field, and proposition bets.

ROULETTE

Roulette is a casino game that uses a perfectly balanced wheel with 38 numbers (0, 00, and 1 through 36), a small white ball, a large layout with 11 different betting options, and special "wheel chips." The layout organizes 11 different bets into 6 "inside bets" (the single numbers, or those closest to the dealer) and 5 "outside bets" (the grouped bets, or those closest to the players).

The dealer spins the wheel clockwise and the ball counterclockwise. When the ball slows, the dealer announces, "No more bets." The ball drops from the "back track" to the "bottom track," caroming off built-in brass barriers and bouncing in and out of the different cups in the wheel before settling into the cup of the winning number. Then the dealer places a marker on the number and scoops all the losing chips into her corner. Depending on how crowded the game is, the casino can count on roughly 50 spins of the wheel per hour.

How to Play

To buy in, place your cash on the layout near the wheel. Inform the dealer of the denomination of the individual unit you intend to play. Know the table limits (displayed on a sign in the dealer area). Don't ask for a 25¢ denomination if the minimum is $1. The dealer gives you a stack of wheel chips of a color that is different from those of all the other players and places a chip marker atop one of your wheel chips on the rim of the wheel to identify its denomination. Note that you must cash in your wheel chips at the roulette table before you leave the game. Only the dealer can verify how much they're worth.

Roulette Strategy

INSIDE BETS

With inside bets, you can lay any number of chips (depending on the table limits) on a single number, 1 through 36 or 0 or 00. If the number hits, your payoff is 35 to 1, for a return of $36. You could, conceivably, place a $1 chip on all 38 numbers, but the return of $36 would leave you $2 short, which divides out to 5.26%, the house advantage. If you place a chip on the line between two numbers and one of those numbers hits, you're paid 17 to 1 for a return of $18 (again, $2 short of the true odds). Betting on three numbers returns 11 to 1, four numbers returns 8 to 1, five numbers pays 6 to 1 (this is the worst bet at roulette, with a 7.89% disadvantage), and six numbers pays 5 to 1.

OUTSIDE BETS

To place an outside bet, lay a chip on one of three "columns" at the lower end of the layout next to numbers 34, 35, and 36. This pays 2 to 1. A bet placed in the first 12, second 12, or third 12 boxes also pays 2 to 1. A bet on red or black, odd or even, and 1 through 18 or 19 through 36 pays off at even money, 1 to 1. If you think you can bet on red *and* black, or odd *and* even, in order to play roulette and drink for free all night, think again. The green 0 or 00, which fall outside these two basic categories, will come up on average once every 19 spins of the wheel.

SLOT MACHINES

Around the turn of 20th century, Charlie Fey built the first slot in his San Francisco basement. Today hundreds of models accept everything from pennies to specially minted $500 tokens. The major advance in the game is the progressive jackpot. Banks of slots within a casino are connected by computer, and the jackpot total is displayed on a digital meter above the machines. Generally, the total increases by 5% of the wager. If you're playing a dollar machine, each time you pull the handle (or press the spin button), a nickel is added to the jackpot.

How to Play

To play, insert your penny, nickel, quarter, silver dollar, or dollar token into the slot at the far right edge of the machine. Pull the handle or press the spin button, and then wait for the reels to spin and stop one by one, and for the machine to determine whether you're a winner (occasionally) or a loser (the rest of the time). It's pretty simple, but because there are so many types of machines nowadays, be sure you know exactly how the one you're playing operates.

Slot-Machine Strategy

The house advantage on slots varies from machine to machine, between 3% and 25%. Casinos that advertise a 97% payback are telling you that at least one of their slot machines has a house advantage of 3%. Which one? There's really no way of knowing. Generally, $1 machines pay back at a higher percentage than quarter or nickel machines. On the other hand, machines with smaller jackpots pay back more money more frequently, meaning that you'll be playing with more of your winnings.

One of the all-time great myths about slot machines is that they're "due" for a jackpot. Slots, like roulette, craps, keno, and Big Six, are subject to the Law of Independent Trials, which means the odds are permanently and unalterably fixed. If the odds of lining up three sevens on a 25¢ slot machine have been set by the casino at 1 in 10,000, then those odds remain 1 in 10,000 whether the three 7s have been hit three times in a row or not hit for 90,000 plays. Don't waste a lot of time playing a machine that you suspect is "ready," and don't think if someone hits a jackpot on a particular machine only minutes after you've finished playing on it that it was "yours."

VIDEO POKER

Like blackjack, video poker is a game of strategy and skill, and at select times on select machines, the player actually holds the advantage, however slight, over the house. Unlike with slot machines, you can determine the exact edge of video poker machines. Like slots, however, video poker machines are often tied into a progressive meter; when the jackpot total reaches high enough, you can beat the casino at its own game. The variety of video poker machines is growing steadily. All are played in similar fashion, but the strategies are different. This section deals only with straight-draw video poker.

How to Play

The schedule for the payback on winning hands is posted on the machine, usually above the screen. It lists the returns for a high pair (generally jacks or better), two pair, three of a kind, a flush, full house, straight flush, four of a kind, and royal flush, depending on the number of coins played—usually 1, 2, 3, 4, or 5. Look for machines that pay with a single coin played: 1 coin for "jacks or better" (meaning a pair of jacks, queens, kings, or aces; any other pair is a stiff), 2 coins for two pairs, 3 for three of a kind, 6 for a flush, 9 for a full house, 50 for a straight flush, 100 for four of a kind, and 250 for a royal flush. This is known as a 9/6 machine—one that gives a nine-coin payback for a full house and a six-coin payback for a flush with one coin played. Other machines are known as 8/5 (eight for a full house, five for a flush), 7/5, and 6/5.

You want a 9/6 machine because it gives you the best odds: the return from a standard 9/6 straight-draw machine is 99.5%; you give up only half a percent to the house. An 8/5 machine returns 97.3%. On 6/5 machines, the figure drops to 95.1%, slightly less than roulette. Machines with varying paybacks are scattered throughout the casinos. In some you'll see an 8/5 machine right next to a 9/6, and someone will be blithely playing the 8/5 machine.

As with slot machines, it's optimum to play the maximum number of coins to qualify for the jackpot. You insert five coins into the slot and press the "deal" button. Five cards appear on the screen—say, 5, jack, queen, 5, 9. To hold the pair of 5s, you press the hold buttons under the first and fourth cards. The word "hold" appears underneath the two 5s. You then press the "draw" button (often the same button as "deal") and three new cards appear on the screen—say, 10, jack, 5. You have three 5s. With five coins bet, the machine will give you 15 credits. Now you can press the "max bet" button: five units will be removed from your credits, and five new cards will appear on the screen. You repeat the hold and draw process; if you hit a winning hand, the proper payback will be added to your credits. Those who want coins rather than credit can hit the "cash out" button at any time. Some machines don't have credit counters and automatically dispense coins for a winning hand.

Video Poker Strategy

Like blackjack, video poker has a basic strategy that's been formulated by the computer simulation of hundreds of millions of hands. The most effective way to learn it is with a video poker computer program that deals the cards on your screen, then tutors you in how to play each hand properly. If you don't want to devote that much time to the study of video poker, memorizing these six rules will help you make the right decision for more than half the hands you'll be dealt:

If you're dealt a completely "stiff" hand (no like cards and no picture cards), draw five new cards.

If you're dealt a hand with no like cards but with one jack, queen, king, or ace, always hold on to the picture card; if you're dealt two different picture cards, hold both. But if you're dealt three different picture cards, hold only two (the two of the same suit, if that's an option).

If you're dealt a pair, hold it, no matter the face value.

Never hold a picture card with a pair of 2s through 10s.

Never draw two cards to try for a straight or a flush.

Never draw one card to try for an inside straight.

Clouds fill the sky and a cool breeze blows as the boat arrives to pick up a group of snorkelers. They board reluctantly, and their hopes of having an underwater adventure dim as the skies open in a dramatic downpour. The boat's bartenders mix up some "captain's specials" and turn the island music up a notch. This elicits smiles all around, and the skies seem to brighten. In no time, the sun is shining again.

IN THIS CHAPTER

outdoor activities
and sports

ABOVE THE SURFACE AND BELOW, Aruban waters are brimming with activity. Although beach bumming is a popular pastime, golf, tennis, and horseback riding are also good options. More adventurous souls can explore the terrain on a motorcycle, parasail with the ocean breezes, or leap through the air on a skydive. Constant trade winds have made Aruba an internationally recognized windsurfing destination. The crystalline waters of the island's leeward side offer scuba divers and snorkelers a kaleidoscopic adventure day or night.

You probably won't find Arubans singing "Take Me Out to the Ball Game," but come time for soccer season (late May–November, with matches on Tuesday, Thursday, Saturday, and Sunday) or track-and-field meets and some 3,200 spirited people pack into the ♻ **COMPLEHO DEPORTIVO G. P. TRINIDAD** (Stadionweg, Oranjestad, tel. 297/582–7488). Events at this complex open with the Aruban national anthem, a display of flags, and the introduction of any old-timers in the stadium. Adult admission ranges from $3 to $6, depending on whether it's a local or international competition; children get in for just over a dollar. Regardless of what's on, you won't find vendors hawking hot dogs or cotton candy. The snack bar sells such Aruban favorites as *pastechi* (meat-, cheese-, or seafood-filled turnovers) or *bitterballen* (bite-size meatballs) that you can wash down with a soda or a local Balashi beer.

Sidney Ponson: Pitcher

When he was growing up in Aruba, Sidney Ponson loved sailing, scuba diving, and just about anything to do with the ocean. "My life was the beach," says Ponson, "before baseball." He started playing baseball when he was 9, even though the game was pretty difficult on an arid island where the fields are full of rocks. But employment on his uncle's boat taught him to work hard for what he wanted in life.

The pitcher signed with the minor leagues at 16, then was tapped by the Baltimore Orioles by the time he was 21. Hitting the big leagues involved lots of hard work (his grueling workouts last from 7:30 AM to 1 PM and involve lifting weights, running, and throwing), but Ponson says it was worth it when he got the call to play. "It was 6:30 AM, and I was on a road trip in a hotel in Scranton," he remembers. "They told me when to show up and said to be ready to play at 8:30."

Now, Ponson spends 10 months a year in the United States pitching for the Orioles and two months in Aruba resting and visiting family and friends. Ponson uses his status as a major leaguer to do some good for his island. He and a fellow Aruban, Calvin Maduro of the Los Angeles Dodgers, draft other professional baseball players, including Pedro Martinez and Manny Ramirez, to play in an annual celebrity softball game to raise funds for Aruba's Cas pa Hubentud, a home for underprivileged children.

To prepare for a game, Ponson heads to the clubhouse for some serious stretching to the hard-rock music of Metallica, AC/DC, or Mötley Crüe. How does it feel right before he heads out to pitch? "One million people want to do what I do—play ball in front of 50,000 people every night," says Ponson, "and that's a great feeling."

BEACHES

The beaches on Aruba are legendary: white sand, turquoise waters, and virtually no litter—everyone takes the NO TIRA SUSHI (NO LITTERING) signs very seriously, especially considering the island's $280 fine. The major public beaches, which back up to the hotels along the southwestern strip, are usually crowded. Make sure you're well protected from the sun—it scorches fast despite the cooling trade winds. Luckily, there's at least one covered bar (and often an ice cream stand) at virtually every hotel. On the island's northeastern side, stronger winds make the waters too choppy for swimming, but the vistas are great and the terrain is wonderful for exploring.

ARASHI BEACH. The water is calm, the swimming is fine, and the white, powdery sands are shaded by some huts (though there are no other facilities). The beach is a 10-minute walk from the last bus stop on Malmok Beach and is accessible by car or taxi.

★ ☺ **BABY BEACH.** On the island's eastern tip, this semicircular beach borders a bay that's as placid and just about as shallow as a wading pool—perfect for tots, shore divers, and terrible swimmers. Thatched shaded areas are good for cooling off. Stop by the nearby snack truck for burgers, hot dogs, beer, and soda.

BOCA CATALINA. Although there are some stones and pebbles along this white-sand beach, snorkelers come for the shallow water filled with fish. Swimmers will also appreciate the calm conditions. There aren't any facilities nearby, however, so pack provisions.

BOCA GRANDI. Strong swimming skills are a must at this beach near the island's eastern tip.

BOCA PRINS. You'll need a four-wheel-drive vehicle to make the trek here. The beach is about as large as a Brazilian bikini, but people don't come here to swim. With two rocky cliffs and crashing waves, it's as romantic as you can imagine. Boca Prins is also famous for its backdrop of enormous vanilla-sand dunes. Bring a picnic, a beach blanket, and sturdy sneakers, and descend the rocks that form steps to the water's edge.

BOCA TABLA. This east-side beach, also known as Bachelor's Beach, is known for the white-powder sand and the good snorkeling and windsurfing. Don't head here for the swimming (conditions aren't the best) or the facilities (there aren't any).

COCO'S BEACH. Next to Baby Beach on the island's eastern tip, this is a beautiful curving stretch of sand only slightly marred by the view of the oil refinery at the bay's far side. Swimming conditions are excellent here, as demonstrated by the local kids diving off the piers. The snack bar at the water's edge has beach equipment rentals and a shop. Local bands play Sunday nights from Easter through summer.

DOS PLAYA. Hire a four-wheel-drive vehicle, pack a blanket and a picnic basket, and head here to take in the beautiful view. Swimming is discouraged because of strong currents and massive waves.

DRUIF. Fine white sand and calm water make this "tops-optional" beach a fine choice for sunbathing and swimming. Convenience is a highlight, too: hotels are close at hand, and the beach is accessible by bus as well as rental car or taxi.

EAGLE BEACH. On the southwestern coast, across the highway from what is quickly becoming known as Time-Share Lane, is what was designated one of the world's best beaches in 2001 by the authors of *Dream Beaches of the World*. Not long ago it was a nearly deserted stretch of pristine sand dotted with the occasional thatched picnic hut. Now that the resorts are completed, this mile-plus-long beach is always hopping.

FISHERMAN'S HUTS. This beach, also called Hadikurari, is a windsurfer's haven. In fact, it's the site for the annual Hi-Winds

Pro-Am Windsurfing Competition. But any day you can take a picnic lunch (tables are available) and watch the elegant purple, aqua, and orange sails catching the breeze. The swimming conditions are good here as well, though the sand has some pebbles and stones.

GRAPEFIELD BEACH. To the northeast of San Nicolas, this sweep of blinding white sand in the shadow of cliffs and boulders is marked by a memorial shaped like an anchor, dedicated to all seamen. Pick sea grapes in high season (January–June). Swim at your own risk, as the waves here can be rough.

MALMOK BEACH. On the northwestern shore, this small, nondescript beach (where some of Aruba's wealthiest families have built residences) borders shallow waters that stretch 300 yards from shore. It's the perfect place to learn to windsurf. Right off the coast here is a favorite haunt for divers and snorkelers— the wreck of the German ship *Antilla*, scuttled in 1940.

MANCHEBO BEACH. In front of the Manchebo Beach Resort, this impressively wide stretch of white powder, also called Punta Brabo, is where officials turn a blind eye to the occasional topless sunbathers.

MANGEL HALTO. Drive or cab it over to this east-side beach, also known as Savaneta. It's a lovely setting for a picnic. Hop into the shallow waters for a swim after taking in the sun on the fine white sand.

PALM BEACH. This stretch runs from the Wyndham Aruba Beach Resort & Casino to the Marriott's Aruba Ocean Club. It's the center of Aruban tourism, offering the best in swimming, sailing, and other water sports. In some spots you might find a variety of shells that are great to collect, but not as much fun to step on barefoot—bring sandals just in case.

SANTO LARGO. Swimming conditions are good—thanks to shallow water edged by white powder sand—but there are no facilities at this beach west of Mangel Halto.

SURFSIDE. Accessible by public bus, car, or taxi, this beach is the perfect place to swim. It's also conveniently located next to the Havana Beach Club and across the street from the Caribbean Town Beach Resort.

ACTIVITIES

Adventure Games

Paintball aficionados can unite in a messier version of capture the flag. The game is played with air guns that propel biodegradable gelatin capsules that splatter you with water-soluble paint on impact. To win, simply return the opposing team's flag to your own team's station without being hit by a pellet. Games (complete with equipment and protective gear) are run by **EVENTS IN MOTION** (Rancho Daimari, Tanki Leendert 249, Plantage Daimari, tel. 297/587–5675, www.visitaruba.com/ranchodaimari). Games last about two hours, costing $35 per person with a minimum of 10 people. You must make reservations three days in advance.

Biking & Motorcycling

Pedal pushing is a great way to get around the island; the climate is perfect, and the trade winds help keep you cool. **PABLITO'S BIKE RENTAL** (L. G. Smith Blvd. 234, Oranjestad, tel. 297/587–8655) rents mountain bikes for $15 a day.

If you prefer to exert less energy while reaping the rewards of the outdoors, a scooter is a great way to whiz from place to place. Or let your hair down completely and cruise around on a Harley Davidson. **BIG TWIN ARUBA** (L. G. Smith Blvd. 124-A, Oranjestad, tel. 297/582–8660, www.harleydavidson-aruba.com) fulfills every biker's fantasy. With an initial $1,000 deposit, rates are $165 for a day or $110 for a half day. The dealership also sells Harley clothing, accessories, and collectibles. Be sure to pose for a photo next to the classic 1939 Liberator on display in the showroom. The shop is open Monday through Saturday from 9 to 6.

There are plenty of dealers around who will be happy to help you in your motoring pursuits. **DONATA CAR AND CYCLE** (Catiri 59, Tanki Leendert, tel. 297/583–4343) rents motorcycles and mopeds. For scooters and all-terrain vehicles, head to **GEORGE'S CYCLE CENTER** (L. G. Smith Blvd. 124, Oranjestad, tel. 297/993–2202). **SEMVER CYCLE RENTAL** (Noord 22, Noord, tel. 297/586–6851) will help you choose the motorcycle or scooter that matches your experience level and your plans for the day.

If you prefer motoring with folks who are in the know, **DE PALM TOURS** (L. G. Smith Blvd. 142, Oranjestad, tel. 297/582–4400 or 800/766–6016, www.depalm.com) offers four- to eight-hour guided tours on all-terrain vehicles that pass through Arikok National Park en route to Natural Bridge. Prices range from $75 to $100. De Palm also conducts a four-wheel-drive tour called the Aruba Safari, one of the most popular trips on the island. The cost is $59 to $75. These trips give you plenty of time to swim and sometimes include lunch.

Bowling

The **EAGLE BOWLING PALACE** (Sasakiweg, Pos Abou, Oranjestad, tel. 297/583–5038) has 16 lanes, a snack bar, and a cocktail lounge. It opens Monday and Tuesday at 5 PM, the rest of the week at 10 AM, and doesn't close until 2 AM. Children under 12 can bowl until 7 PM. One lane for one hour will cost $10–$12, depending on the time of day.

Fishing

Deep-sea catches here include barracuda, kingfish, blue and white marlin, wahoo, bonito, and black and yellow tuna. Each

October, the island hosts the International White Marlin Competition. Many skippered charter boats are available for half- or full-day sails. Packages include tackle, bait, and refreshments. Prices range from $220 to $320 for a half-day charter and from $400 to $600 for a full day. Contact **DE PALM TOURS** (L. G. Smith Blvd. 142, Oranjestad, tel. 297/582–4400 or 800/766–6016, www.depalm.com) for a choice of fishing excursions. **PELICAN TOURS & WATERSPORTS** (Pelican Pier, near the Holiday Inn and Playa Linda hotels, Palm Beach, tel. 297/586–3271, www.pelican-aruba.com) is not just for the surf and snorkel crowd; the company will help you catch trophy-size fish. **RED SAIL SPORTS** (J. E. Irausquin Blvd. 83, Oranjestad, tel. 297/586–1603, 877/733–7245 in U.S., www.aruba-redsail.com) will arrange everything for your fishing trip. **TEASER CHARTERS** (St. Vincentweg 5, Oranjestad, tel. 297/582–5088, www.teasercharters.com) offers the hook and line, but the sinker is up to you.

Golf

Golf may seem incongruous on an arid island such as Aruba, yet there are popular courses. The constant trade winds and occasional stray goat add unexpected hazards.

The **ARUBA GOLF CLUB** (Golfweg 82, San Nicolas, tel. 297/584–2006) has a 9-hole course with 20 sand traps and 5 water traps, roaming goats, and lots of cacti. There are also 11 greens covered with artificial turf, making 18-hole tournaments a possibility. The clubhouse has a bar and locker rooms. Greens fees are $10 for 9 holes, $15 for 18 holes. Golf carts are available.

ARUBA GOLF & LEISURE (J. E. Irasquin Blvd. 326, Oranjestad, tel. 297/586–4590) has a 300-yard driving range, an 18-hole putting green, and a chipping area. Pay $3 for a bucket of balls and $10 for a half set of rental clubs. It's open from 7 AM to 11 PM daily.

A moat surrounds the pair of elevated 18-hole miniature golf courses at **JOE MENDEZ MINIATURE ADVENTURE GOLF** (Sasakiweg, Noord, tel. 297/587–6625). There are also paddleboats and bumper boats, a snack stand, and a bar. A round of 18 holes costs $6.50. It's open 5 PM to 1 AM during the week and from noon to 1 AM on the weekends.

Golfers can rejoice, because **THE LINKS AT DIVI ARUBA** (J. E. Irasquin Blvd. 93, Oranjestad, tel. 297/525–5200), a 9-hole golf course designed by Karl Litten and Lorie Viola, opened in 2004. The par 36 course on paspalum grass (best for seaside courses) takes you past beautiful lagoons. Amenities include a golf school with professional instruction, a swing analysis station, a driving range, and a two-story golf clubhouse with a pro shop. Two restaurants serving contemporary American cuisine with Caribbean accents are par for the course.

★ On the northwest coast, **TIERRA DEL SOL GOLF COURSE** (Malmokweg, tel. 297/586–0978) is a stunner. Designed by Robert Trent Jones Jr., this 18-hole championship course combines Aruba's native beauty—cacti and rock formations—with the lush greens of the world's best courses. The three knockouts are Hole 3, perched on a cliff overlooking the sea; Hole 14, with a saltwater marsh inhabited by wild egrets; and Hole 16, whose fairway rolls along dunes. The $130 greens fee includes a golf cart equipped with a communications system that allows you to order drinks that will be ready upon your return. Half-day golf clinics, a bargain at $45, include lunch in the clubhouse. The pro shop is one of the Caribbean's most elegant, with an extremely attentive staff. Package vacations with villa rentals are available.

Hiking

There are more than 34 km (20 mi) of trails in **ARIKOK NATIONAL PARK** (tel. 297/582–8001), concentrated in the island's eastern interior and along its northeastern coast. The park is crowned by Aruba's second-highest mountain, the 577-foot Mt. Arikok, so climbing is also a possibility.

Hiking in the park, whether alone or in a group led by guides, is generally not too strenuous. Look for different colors to determine the degree of difficulty of each trail. Sturdy shoes are a must to grip the granular surfaces and climb the occasionally steep terrain. You should also exercise caution with the strong sun—bring along plenty of water and wear sunscreen and a hat.

The Aruban government is working on a 10-year ecotourism plan to preserve the resources of the park, which makes up 18% of the island's total area. The effort includes setting aside areas for recreation, establishing zones where the natural habitats are protected, and developing a scenic loop roadway. At the park's main entrance, the Arikok Center houses offices, rest rooms, and food facilities. Under the new plan, all visitors stop here upon entering so that officials can manage the traffic flow and distribute information on park rules and features.

Horseback Riding

Several ranches offer short jaunts along the beach or longer rides along trails passing through countryside flanked by cacti, divi-divi trees, and aloe vera plants. Ask if you can stop off at Cura di Tortuga, a natural pool that's reputed to have restorative powers. Rides are also possible in the Arikok National Park. Rates run from $25 for an hour-long trip to $65 for a three-hour tour. Private rides cost slightly more.

DE PALM TOURS (L. G. Smith Blvd. 142, Oranjestad, tel. 297/582-4400 or 800/766-6016, www.depalm.com) arranges horseback-riding excursions. **RANCHO DEL CAMPO** (Sombre 22E, Santa Cruz, tel. 297/585-0290, www.ranchodelcampo.com), the first to offer rides to Natural Pool back in 1991, leads excursion for $50 per person. **RANCHO DAIMARI** (Plantage Daimari, tel. 297/587-5674, www.visitaruba.com/ranchodaimari) will lead your horse to water—

Wildlife Watching

Wildlife abounds on Aruba. Look for the cottontail rabbit: the black patch on its neck likens it to a species found in Venezuela, spawning a theory that it was brought to the island by pre-Columbian peoples. Wild donkeys, originally transported to the island by the Spanish, are found in the more rugged terrain; sheep and goats roam freely throughout the island.

About 170 bird species make their home on Aruba year round, and migratory birds temporarily raise the total to 300 species when they fly by in November and January. Among the highlights are the trupiaal (which is bright orange), the prikichi (a parakeet with a green body and yellow head), and the barika geel (a small, yellow-bellied bird with a sweet tooth—you may find one eating the sugar off your breakfast table). At Bubali Bird Sanctuary on the island's western side, you can see various types of waterfowl, especially cormorants, herons, scarlet ibis, and fish eagles. Along the south shore, brown pelicans are common. At Tierra del Sol Golf Course in the north, you may glimpse the shoko, the endangered burrowing owl.

Lizard varieties include large iguanas, once hunted for use in local soups and stews. (That practice is now illegal.) Like chameleons, these iguanas change color to adapt to their surroundings—from bright green when foraging in the foliage (which they love to eat) to a brownish shade when sunning themselves in the dirt. The pega pega—a cousin of the gecko—is named for the suction pads on its feet that allow it to grip virtually any surface (pega means "to stick" in Papiamento). The kododo blauw (whiptail lizard) is one of the species that is unique to the island.

Two types of snakes are found only on Aruba. The cat-eyed santanero isn't venomous, but it won't hesitate to defecate in your hand should you pick it up. The poisonous cascabel is a unique subspecies of rattlesnake that doesn't use its rattle. These snakes live in the area between Mt. Yamanota, Fontein, and San Nicolas.

either at Natural Bridge or Natural Pool—in the morning or afternoon for $55 per person. The "Junior Dudes" program is tailored for young riders. **RANCHO NOTORIOUS** (Boroncana, Noord, tel. 297/586–0508, www.ranchonotorious.com) will take you on a tour of the countryside for $50, to the beach to snorkel for $55, or on a three-hour ride up to the California Lighthouse for $65.

Jet Skiing

For sheer excitement, there's nothing like sputtering around Aruba's aqua-blue water on jet skis. Rentals are available in the water sports centers at most hotels. Average prices for a half-hour ride are $45 for a single jet ski and $55 for a double. There are a few operators on the island, two of which are well regarded. **PELICAN TOURS & WATERSPORTS** (Pelican Pier, near the Holiday Inn and Playa Linda hotels, Palm Beach, tel. 297/586–3271, www.pelican-aruba.com) offers jet skis and wave runners. **UNIQUE SPORTS OF ARUBA** (L. G. Smith Blvd. 79, Oranjestad, tel./fax 297/586–0096 or 297/586–3900, www.visitaruba.com/uniquesports), operating exclusively from the Aruba Grand Beach Resort on Palm Beach, rents single and double jet skis.

Kayaking

Kayaking is a popular sport on Aruba, especially because the waters are so calm. It's a great way to explore the coast. Every day except Sunday, **DE PALM TOURS** (L. G. Smith Blvd. 142, Oranjestad, tel. 297/582–4400 or 800/766–6016, www.depalm.com) offers a four-hour guided kayaking tour that includes some snorkeling. The cost, including lunch, is $77.

Kiteboarding

Thanks to constant trade winds, kiteboarding (also called kitesurfing) is fast becoming a popular pastime on this tiny island. The sport involves gliding on and above the water on a small surfboard or wakeboard while hooked up to an inflatable kite. Windsurfing experience helps, and practice time on the beach is essential. Those eager to fly the friendly skies can take lessons and rent reliable equipment at Vela Windsurf's ★ **FISHERMAN'S HUTS WINDSURF CENTER** (L. G. Smith Blvd. 101, Palm Beach, tel. 297/586–9000 Ext. 6430 or 800/223–5443, www.velawindsurf.com). Another kiteboarding operator is **ARUBA BOARDSAILING PRODUCTIONS** (L. G. Smith Blvd. 486, Palm Beach, tel. 297/586–3940 or 297/993–1111, www.visitaruba.com/arubaboardsailing). If you get the hang of it, you may want to pursue some of the island's freestyle tournaments and long-distance races.

Parasailing

For about 12 exhilarating minutes, motorboats at Palm and Eagle beaches tow you up and over the waters around Aruba ($45 for a single-seater, $75 for a tandem). You can make arrangements with your hotel, or through independent operators stationed on the beaches. **CARIBBEAN PARASAIL** (tel. 297/586–0505) is one of the island's top operators. Working with many hotels, **PELICAN TOURS & WATERSPORTS** (Pelican Pier, near the Holiday Inn and the Playa Linda hotels, Palm Beach, tel. 297/586–3271, www.pelican-aruba.com) has equipment for parasailing and other outdoor activities. Although it's best known for its diving trips, **RED SAIL SPORTS** (J. E. Irausquin Blvd. 83, tel. 297/586–1603, 877/733–7245 in U.S., www.aruba-redsail.com) will also take you parasailing.

Playgrounds

☺ You can let the kids run loose in **KIBAIMA MINIATURE VILLAGE,** (south of the airport across Highway 4 from the outdoor theater) (Kibaima 5, Oranjestad, tel. 297/585–1830 or 297/585–1980, www.arubaexperts.com/arubatourism/tourdetail.asp?EventID=246), a little park filled with scaled-down versions of typical Aruban houses. There are also plenty of exotic birds and animals. The park is open daily from 10 AM to 6 PM, with daily 10 AM tours at a $5 admission charge for children under 12 years old and $10 for adults.

TIRA KOOCHI PARK (Savaneta 338A, Oranjestad) is open daily from 4 PM to 6:30 PM daily. The playground is behind Prome Paso School.

Sailing

You can have a hull of a good time sailing around Aruba on a Sunfish, or you can opt for a daytime or sunset sail aboard a trimaran or catamaran. The **SEAPORT MARINA** (Seaport Marketplace 204, Oranjestad, tel. 297/583–9190, www. seaportmarinaaruba.com) is the place to go for charters.

DE PALM TOURS (L. G. Smith Blvd. 142, Oranjestad, tel. 297/ 582–4400 or 800/766–6016, www.depalm.com) will sail you over the open seas for a two- to four-hour snorkeling adventure at nearby reefs. The cost for the catamaran trip is $37–$59 per person. **MI DUSHI** (Turibana Plaza, Noord 124, Noord, tel. 297/ 586–2010, www.arubaadventures.com), a ship whose name means "My Sweetheart," will sail you into the sunset with yours for $35 per person. Daytime snorkeling trips on this romantic two-masted ship include breakfast, lunch, and drinks for $69 per person. **PELICAN TOURS & WATERSPORTS** (Pelican Pier, near the Holiday Inn and Playa Linda hotels, Palm Beach, tel. 297/ 586–3271, www.pelican-aruba.com) offers daytime snorkeling trips to two different reefs for about $30 per person. The company also offers sunset sails for the same price that can be combined with dinner at the Pelican Restaurant on Palm Beach. **RED SAIL SPORTS** (J. E. Irausquin Blvd. 83, Oranjestad, tel. 297/ 586–1603, 877/733–7245 in U.S., www.aruba-redsail.com) serves you lunch and lets you snorkel at two different sites for $56 per person. There's also a sunset cruise for $35 per person.

Scuba Diving & Snorkeling

With visibility of up to 90 feet, the waters around Aruba are excellent for snorkeling and diving. Both advanced and novice divers will find plenty to occupy their time, as many of the most popular sites, including some interesting shipwrecks, are found in shallow waters ranging from 30 feet to 60 feet. Coral reefs covered with sensuously waving sea fans and eerie giant sponge tubes attract a colorful menagerie of sea life, including gliding manta rays, curious sea turtles, shy octopuses, and fish from grunts to groupers. Note that marine preservation is a priority on Aruba, and regulations by the Conference on International Trade in Endangered Species make it unlawful to remove coral, conch, and other marine life from the water.

Most resorts offer diving courses for beginners that include instruction and all equipment; those seeking advanced certification can do so through any of the island's licensed dive centers. Some popular dive sites are listed below, but be sure to pick up the Aruba Tourism Authority's brochure, "The Island for Water Sports," which describes many more.

OPERATORS

Expect snorkel gear to rent for about $15 per day and snorkeling trips to cost around $40. Scuba rates are around $50 for a one-tank reef or wreck dive, $65 for a two-tank dive, and $45 for a night dive. Resort courses, which offer an introduction to scuba diving, average $65 to $70. If you want to go all the way, complete open-water certification costs around $300.

The more seasoned diving crowd might check with **ARUBA PRO DIVE** (Ponton 88, Noord, tel. 297/582–5520, www.arubaprodive.com) for special deals. **DAX DIVERS** (Kibaima 7, Santa Cruz, tel. 297/585–1270) has an instructor training course. Some dives are less expensive, at $40 for 40 minutes with one tank and weights. **DE PALM TOURS** (L. G. Smith Blvd. 142, Oranjestad, tel. 297/582–4400 or 800/766–6016) is one of the best options for your undersea experience, and the options go beyond basic diving. Don a helmet and walk along the ocean floor near De Palm Island, home of huge blue parrot fish. Have your picture taken at an underwater table loaded with champagne glasses and roses. Try Snuba—like scuba diving but without the heavy air tanks—either from a boat or from an island. It's $55 when you book another activity. **DIVE ARUBA** (Williamstraat 8, Oranjestad, tel. 297/582–4554, www.divearuba.com) offers resort courses, certification courses, and trips to interesting shipwrecks. At Manchebo Beach Resort, **MERMAID SPORT DIVERS** (J. E. Irausquin Blvd. 55A, Eagle Beach, tel. 297/587–4103, www.scubadivers-aruba.com) has dive packages with PADI-certified instructors.

NATIVE DIVERS ARUBA (Koyari 1, Noord, tel. 297/586–4763, www.nativedivers.com) offers all types of dives. Courses in specialties such as underwater naturalist are taught by PADI-certified instructors. **PELICAN TOURS & WATERSPORTS** (Pelican Pier, near the Holiday Inn and Playa Linda hotels, Palm Beach, tel. 297/586–3271, www.pelican-aruba.com) has options for divers of all levels. Novices start with midmorning classes and then move to the pool to practice what they've learned; by afternoon they put their new skills to use at a shipwreck off the coast. **RED SAIL SPORTS** (J. E. Irausquin Blvd. 83, Oranjestad, tel. 297/586–1603, 877/733–7245 in U.S., www.aruba-redsail.com) has courses for children and others new to scuba diving. An introductory class costs about $80.

SEARUBA FLY 'N DIVE (Shiribana 9A, Paradera, tel. 297/587–8759, www.searuba.com) will take you higher and lower than you ever thought possible in one day. You can take aerial shots from above the dive sites, then dive underwater. Aside from the usual diving courses, the company will instruct your group in rescue techniques for around $350 per person. At the Aruba Grand Beach Resort, **UNIQUE SPORTS OF ARUBA** (L. G. Smith Blvd. 79, Oranjestad, tel. 297/586–0096 or 297/586–3900, www.visitaruba.com/uniquesports) lives up to its name, providing dive master, rescue, and certification courses.

WEST SIDE DIVE SITES

ANTILLA WRECK. This German freighter, which sank off the northwest coast near Malmok Beach, is very popular with both divers and snorkelers. Scuttled during World War II not long after its maiden voyage, the 400-foot-long vessel—referred to by locals as "the ghost ship"—has large compartments. You can climb into the captain's bathtub, which sits beside the wreck, for a unique photo op. Lobster, angelfish, yellowtail, and other fish swim about the wreck, which is blanketed by giant tube sponges and coral.

BARCADERA REEF. Only large types of coral—staghorn, elkhorn, pillar—find their niche close to this reef because the sand makes it difficult for the smaller varieties to survive. The huge (and abundant) sea fans here wave in the current.

BLACK BEACH. The clear waters just off this beach are dotted with sea fans. The area takes its name from the rounded black stones lining the shore. It's the only bay on the island's north coast sheltered from thunderous waves, making it a safe spot for diving.

CALIFORNIAN WRECK. Although this steamer is submerged at a depth that's perfect for underwater photography, this site is safe only for advanced divers; the currents here are strong, and the waters are dangerously choppy.

HARBOUR REEF. Steeply sloped boulders surrounded by a multitude of soft coral formations make this a great spot for novices. The calm waters are noteworthy for their abundance of fascinating plant life.

MALMOK REEF. Lobsters and stingrays are among the highlights at this bottom reef adorned by giant green, orange, and purple barrel sponges as well as leaf and brain coral. From here you can spot the *Debbie II*, a 120-foot barge that sank in 1992.

PEDERNALES WRECK. During World War II, this oil tanker was torpedoed by a German submarine. The U.S. military cut out the damaged centerpiece, towed the two remaining pieces to the States, and welded them together into a smaller vessel that eventually transported troops during the invasion of Normandy. The section that was left behind in shallow water is now surrounded by coral formations, making this a good site for novice divers. The ship's cabins, washbasins, and pipelines are exposed. The area teems with grouper and angelfish.

SKELETON CAVE. Human bones found here (historians hypothesize that they're remains of ancient Arawak people) gave this dive spot its name. A large piece of broken rock forms the entrance where the cave meets the coast.

SONESTA REEF. Two downed planes are the centerpiece of this interesting dive site near Sonesta Island. Several types of brain coral abound in this sandy-bottom area.

TUGBOAT WRECK. Spotted eagle rays and stingrays are sometimes observed at this shipwreck at the foot of Harbour Reef, making it one of Aruba's most popular. Spectacular formations of brain, sheet, and star coral blanket the path to the wreck, which is inhabited by a pair of bright green moray eels.

EAST SIDE DIVE SITES
CAPTAIN ROGER WRECK. A plethora of colorful fish swish about this old tugboat, which rests off the coast at Seroe Colorado. From shore you can swim to a steep coral reef.

ISLA DI ORO. A wide expanse of reef grows far out along the shallow bank, making for superb diving. You'll be treated to views of green moray eels, coral crabs, trumpet fish, and French, gray, and queen angelfish.

JANE WRECK. This 200-foot freighter, lodged in an almost vertical position at a depth of 90 feet, is near the coral reef west of Palm Island. Night diving is exciting here, as the polyps emerge from the corals that grow profusely on the steel plates of the decks and cabins. Soft corals and sea fans are also abundant in the area.

PALM ISLAND. Secluded behind clusters of mangrove, the reef system around Palm Island stretches all the way to Oranjestad. You can get close enough to touch the nurse sharks that sleep tucked into reef crevices during the day.

PUNTA BASORA. This narrow reef stretches far into the sea off the island's easternmost point. On calm days you'll see eagle rays, stingrays, barracudas, and hammerhead sharks, as well as hawksbill and loggerhead turtles.

SHARK CAVES. At this site along the island's southeastern point you can swim alongside sand sharks and float past the nurse sharks sleeping under the rock outcroppings.

VERA WRECK. In 1954, this freighter sank while en route to North America. The crew, saved by an Aruban captain, claimed the ship held Nazi treasures.

THE WALL. From May to August, green sea turtles intent on laying their eggs abound at this steep-walled reef. You'll also spot long-branched gorgons, groupers, and burrfish swimming nearby. Close to shore, massive sheet corals are plentiful; in the upper part of the reef are colorful varieties such as black coral, star coral, and flower coral. Flitting about are brilliant damselfish, rock beauties, and porgies.

Skydiving

You can fall head over heels for Aruba as you leap out of an airplane at 10,000 feet. Tandem jumps are offered early in the morning seven days a week by **SKYDIVE ARUBA** (Paradera 211, Paradera, tel. 297/993–7151). To make the leap, you must be over 18 years old, less than 240 pounds, and in good health. This remarkable two-hour experience costs $220.

Tennis

Aruba's winds make tennis a challenge even if you have the best of backhands. Although visitors can make arrangements to play at the resorts, priority goes to guests. Some private tennis clubs can also accommodate you. Try the facilities at the **ARUBA RACQUET CLUB** (Rooisanto 21, Palm Beach, tel. 297/586–0215). Host to a variety of international tournaments, the club has eight courts (six lighted), as well as a swimming pool, an aerobics center, and a restaurant. Fees are $10 per hour; a lesson with a pro costs $20 for a half hour, $40 for one hour.

Windsurfing

Whisk through the waves and revel in the sea spray. Aruba has all it takes for windsurfing: trade winds that average 15 knots year-round (peaking May–July), a sunny climate, and perfect azure-blue waters. With a few lessons from a certified instructor, even novices will be jibing in no time. The southwestern coast's tranquil waters make it ideal for both beginners and intermediates, as the winds are steady but sudden gusts rare. Experts will find the waters of the Atlantic, especially around Grapefield and Boca Grandi beaches, more challenging; winds are fierce and often shift without warning. Rentals average about $60 a day, and lessons range from $45 to $75. Many hotels include windsurfing in their water sports packages, and most operators can help you arrange complete windsurfing vacations.

Every June sees the Hi-Winds Pro-Am Windsurfing Competition, attracting professionals and amateurs from around the world. There are divisions for women, men, juniors, masters, and grand masters. Disciplines include slalom, course racing, long distance, and freestyle. The entry fee is $150, but there's a $25 discount if you register online at www.aruba-hiwinds.com.

ARUBA BEACH VILLAS (L. G. Smith Blvd. 462, Malmok Beach, tel. 297/586–2527, 800/320–9998 in U.S., www.arubasailboardvacations.com) offers first-rate instruction. It's at Windsurf Village, a lodging complex created by and for windsurfers near Fisherman's Huts, a world-renowned sailing spot. Another lure for those in the know: the complex is home to one of the Caribbean's largest and best-stocked windsurfing shops.

Trade jokes and snap photos with your fellow windsurfers at Vela Windsurf's **FISHERMAN'S HUTS WINDSURF CENTER** (L. G. Smith Blvd. 101 Palm Beach, tel. 297/586–9000 Ext. 6430 or 800/223–5443, www.velawindsurf.com), at the north end of the Marriott Hotel property in front of the Fisherman's Huts. This is the place to make friends on the water. **PELICAN TOURS & WATERSPORTS** (Pelican Pier, near the Holiday Inn and Playa Linda hotels, Palm Beach, tel. 297/586–3271, www.pelican-aruba.com) usually has boards and sails on hand. The day will fly by when you windsurf with **SAILBOARD VACATIONS** (L. G. Smith Blvd. 462, Malmok Beach, tel. 297/586–2527, www.sailboardvacations.com).

Hooiberg loomed before the adventure seeker. Water bottle in hand, he gingerly began his ascent. His breath grew shorter as he made his way up the 562 steps. Within 15 minutes he reached the top and paused to take in a view that stretched all the way to Venezuela. Leonardo DiCaprio's line in Titanic flashed through his mind: "I'm the king of the world!" On the way down, he encountered a group about to embark on the same journey. "Piece of cake," he offered, nodding toward the hill. Then he headed back to his hotel for a massage.

IN THIS CHAPTER

here and there

ARUBA'S WILDLY SCULPTED LANDSCAPE is replete with rocky deserts, cactus clusters, secluded coves, blue vistas, and the trademark divi-divi tree. To preserve the environment while encouraging visitors to explore, the government has implemented a 10-year, $10 million ecotourism plan. Initiatives include finding ways to make efficient use of the limited land resources and protecting the natural and cultural resources in such preserves as Arikok National Park and the Coastal Protection Zone (along the island's north and east coasts).

Oranjestad, Aruba's capital, is good for shopping by day and dining by night, but the "real Aruba"—with its untamed beauty—can be found only in the countryside. Rent a car, take a sightseeing tour, or hire a cab for $30 an hour. Though desolate, the northern and eastern shores are striking and well worth a visit. A drive out past the California Lighthouse or to Seroe Colorado will give you a feel for the backcountry.

Although the main highways are well paved, the windward side of the island still has some roads that are a mixture of compacted dirt and stones. A car is fine, but a four-wheel-drive vehicle will enable you to better navigate the unpaved interior. Remember that few beaches outside the hotel strip along Palm and Eagle beaches to the west have refreshment stands, so pack your own food and drink. Aside from those in the infrequent restaurant, there are no public bathrooms outside of Oranjestad.

Traffic is sparse, but signs leading to sights are often small and hand lettered (this is slowly changing as the government puts up official road signs), so watch closely. Route 1A travels southbound along the western coast, and 1B is simply northbound along the same road. If you lose your way, just follow the divi-divi trees.

Numbers in the margin correspond to points of interest on the Exploring map.

WESTERN ARUBA

Western Aruba is where you'll likely spend most of your time. All the resorts and time-shares are along this coast, most of them clustered on the oceanfront strip at the luscious Palm and Eagle beaches, in the city of Oranjestad, or in the district of Noord. All the casinos, major shopping malls, and most restaurants are found in this region, as is the airport.

A Good Tour

Rent a car and head out on Route 1A toward **ORANJESTAD** ① for some sightseeing and shopping. Pick up Route 1B out of town. At a large roundabout turn right and drive for about 1 km (½ mi), then make another right at the first intersection and drive for ½ km (¼ mi) until you reach the fields and factory of **ARUBA ALOE** ②. Head back to the roundabout and pick up Route 4A. Follow this road a short way to the **AYO AND CASIBARI ROCK FORMATIONS** ③. Continue on 4A and follow the signs for **HOOIBERG** ④; if you're so inclined, climb the steps of Haystack Hill. Return on 4B to 6A and drive a couple of miles to the Bushiribana Gold Smelter. Beyond it on the windward coast is the **NATURAL BRIDGE** ⑤. You'll have to veer off 6A, which bends east here; follow the signs.

Retrace your drive to Route 6; take 6B to the intersection of Route 3B, which you'll follow into the town of **NOORD** ⑥, a good place to stop for lunch. Then take Route 2B, following the signs for the branch road leading to the **ALTO VISTA CHAPEL** ⑦.

Return to town and pick up 2B and then 1B to reach the **CALIFORNIA LIGHTHOUSE** ⑧. In this area you'll also see Arashi Beach (a popular snorkeling site) and the Tierra Del Sol golf course. From the lighthouse follow 1A back toward Palm Beach. On the way, stop at the **BUTTERFLY FARM** ⑨ and the **BUBALI BIRD SANCTUARY** ⑩.

TIMING
If you head out right after breakfast, you can just about complete the tour above in one very full day. If you want to linger in Oranjestad's shops or go snorkeling along the beach, consider breaking the tour up into two days.

What to See

⑦ **ALTO VISTA CHAPEL.** On the island's northwest corner, amid eerie boulders and looming cacti, sits the little Alto Vista Chapel. The wind whistles through the simple mustard-color walls. Along the side of the road back to civilization are miniature crosses depicting the stations of the cross and hand-lettered signs exhorting PRAY FOR US SINNERS and the like—a simple yet powerful evocation of faith. To get here, follow the rough, winding dirt road that loops around the island's northern tip. From the hotel strip, take Palm Beach Road through three intersections and watch for the asphalt road to the left just past the Alto Vista Rum Shop.

★ ② **ARUBA ALOE.** Learn all about this fascinating substance—its cultivation, processing, and production—at Aruba's own aloe farm and factory. Guided tours lasting about half an hour will show you how the gel—revered for its skin-soothing properties—is extracted from the aloe vera plant and used in a variety of products, including after-sun creams, soaps, and shampoos. You can purchase the finished goods in the gift shop. *Pitastraat 115, Oranjestad, tel. 297/588–3222, www.arubaaloe.com. $6. Weekdays 8:30–4:30, Sat. 9–2.*

exploring

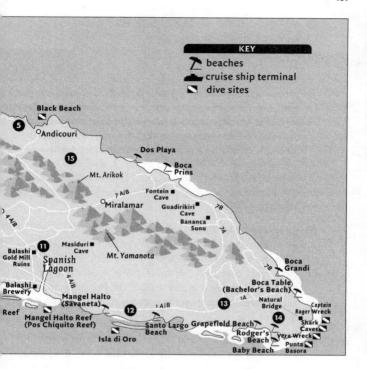

KEY
🏖 beaches
⚓ cruise ship terminal
◣ dive sites

Black Beach
⑤
○ Andicouri

Dos Playa

Boca Prins

⑮

Mt. Arikok

7 A|B

Fontein Cave

○ Miralamar

Guadirikiri Cave

Bananca Sunu

7 B

4 A|B

Balashi Gold Mill Ruins
⑪
Masiduri Cave

Spanish Lagoon

Mt. Yamanota

7 A

Boca Grandi

7 B

Balashi Brewery

4 A|B

Mangel Halto (Savaneta)
⑫

Boca Table (Bachelor's Beach)

1 A

Natural Bridge

⑬

Captain Roger Wreck

Reef

Mangel Halto Reef (Pos Chiquito Reef)

1 A|B

Santo Largo Beach

Grapefield Beach

⑭

Shark Caves

Isla di Oro

Rodger's Beach

Vera Wreck

Baby Beach

Punta Basora

❸ AYO AND CASIBARI ROCK FORMATIONS. The massive boulders at Ayo and Casibari are a mystery, as they don't match the island's geological makeup. You can climb to the top for fine views of the arid countryside. On the way you'll doubtless pass Aruba whiptail lizards—the males are cobalt blue, the females blue with dots. The main path to Casibari has steps and handrails (except on one side), and you must move through tunnels and along narrow steps and ledges to reach the top. At Ayo you'll find ancient pictographs in a small cave (the entrance has iron bars to protect the drawings from vandalism). You may also encounter boulder climbers, who are increasingly drawn to Ayo's smooth surfaces. Access to Casibari is via Tanki Highway 4A to Ayo via Route 6A; watch carefully for the turnoff signs near the center of the island on the way to the windward side.

❿ BUBALI BIRD SANCTUARY. Bird-watchers delight in the more than 80 species of migratory birds that nest in this wetlands area inland from the island's strip of high-rise hotels. Herons, egrets, cormorants, coots, gulls, skimmers, terns, and ducks are among the winged wonders in and around the two interconnected artificial lakes that compose the sanctuary. *J. E. Irausquin Blvd., Noord, No phone. Free.*

★ ◔ ❾ **BUTTERFLY FARM.** Hundreds of butterflies from around the world flutter by at this spectacular garden. Guided 20- to 30-minute tours (included in the price of admission) provide an entertaining look into how these creatures complete their life cycle: from egg to caterpillar to chrysalis to butterfly. Pay once and you can visit as many times as you like for the duration of your trip. *J. E. Irausquin Blvd., Palm Beach, tel. 297/586-3656, www.thebutterflyfarm.com. $12. Daily 9–4:30 (last tour at 4).*

❽ CALIFORNIA LIGHTHOUSE. This lighthouse, built by a French architect in 1910, stands at the island's far northern end. Although the interior is closed to the public, you can ascend the hill to its base for some great views. In this stark landscape you'll feel as though you've just landed on the moon. The structure is surrounded by huge boulders that look like extraterrestrial monsters and sand dunes embroidered with scrub that resemble undulating sea serpents. Next to the nearby Trattoria El Farro Blanco—a great place to watch the sun set—there's a placard explaining the lighthouse's history and telling of the wreck of a German ship just offshore.

④ **HOOIBERG.** Named for its unusual shape (*hooiberg* means "haystack" in Dutch), this 541-foot peak lies inland just past the airport. Climb the 562 steps to the top for an impressive view of the city of Oranjestad. On a clear day, you can even see the northern coast of Venezuela.

⑤ **NATURAL BRIDGE.** Centuries of raging tides sculpted this coral rock bridge in the center of the windward coast. To reach it, drive inland along Hospitalstraat and then follow the signs. Just before you reach the geological wonder, you'll pass the massive stone ruins of the Bushiribana Gold Smelter, an intriguing structure that resembles a crumbling fortress, and a section of surf-pounded coastline called Boca Mahos. Near Natural Bridge are a souvenir shop and a café overlooking the water.

⑥ **NOORD.** The district of Noord is home to the strip of high-rise hotels and casinos that line Palm Beach. Here you'll also find the beautiful St. Ann's Church, known for its ornate 19th-century altar. In this area, Aruban-style homes are scattered amid clusters of cacti.

① **ORANJESTAD.** Aruba's charming capital is best explored on foot. Its palm-lined central thoroughfare runs between old and new pastel-painted buildings of typical Dutch design (Spanish influence is also evident in some of the architecture). There are many malls with boutiques and shops; downtown and Seaport Village are the major shopping areas. Every morning, the wharf teems with activity as merchants sell produce and fresh fish—often right off their boats. You can also buy handicrafts and T-shirts at this dockside bazaar, where bargaining is expected and dollars or

The Divi-Divi Tree

Like a statuesque dancer in a graceful flat-back pose, the watapana, or divi-divi tree, is one of Aruba's hallmarks. Oddly enough, this tropical shrub is a member of the legume family. Its astringent pods contain high levels of tannin, which is leached out for tanning leather. The pods also yield a black dye. The tree has a moderate rate of growth and a high drought tolerance. Typically it reaches no more than 25 feet in height, with a flattened crown and irregular, forked branches. Its leaves are dull green, and its inconspicuous yet fragrant flowers are pale yellow or white and grow in small clusters. Thanks to constant trade winds, the divi-divis serve as a natural compass: they're bent toward the island's leeward—or western—side, where most of the hotels are.

florins are accepted. Island schooners and houseboats anchored near the fishing boats add to the port's ambience. Wilhelmina Park, a small tropical garden on the waterfront along L. G. Smith Boulevard, has a sculpture of the Netherlands' Queen Wilhelmina, whose reign lasted from 1890 to 1948.

At the **Archaeological Museum of Aruba** you'll find two rooms chock-full of fascinating artifacts from the indigenous Arawak people, including farm and domestic utensils dating back hundreds of years. J. E. Irausquinplein 2A, tel. 297/582–8979. Free. Weekdays 8–noon and 1–4.

One of the island's oldest edifices, **Fort Zoutman** was built in 1796 and played an important role in skirmishes between British and Curaçao troops in 1803. The Willem III Tower, named for the Dutch monarch of that time, was added in 1868 to serve as a lighthouse. Over time, the fort has been put to use as a government office building, a police station, and a prison. Now its historical museum displays Aruban artifacts in an 18th-century house. *Zoutmanstraat, tel. 297/582–6099. Free. Weekdays 8–noon and 1–4.*

★ The **Numismatic Museum** displays more than 40,000 historic coins and paper money from around the world. A few pieces were salvaged from shipwrecks in the region. Some of the coins circulated during the Roman Empire, the Byzantine Empire, and the ancient Chinese dynasties; the oldest dates to the 3rd century BC. The museum—which moved in 2003 to a new, larger location next to the central bus station—had its start as the private collection of one Aruban who dug up some old coins in his garden. It is now run by his granddaughter. *Westraat, tel. 297/582–8831. Free. Mon.–Thurs. 9–4, Fri. 9–1, Sat. 9–noon.*

☺ The **Experience Aruba Panorama** brings the island's history and culture to life in a 22-minute cinematic extravaganza that fills five massive screens measuring 13 feet high and 66 feet wide. The breathtaking shows begin in the Crystal Theater at the Renaissance Aruba Beach Resort every hour from 11 to 5. *L. G. Smith Blvd. 82 Oranjestad, tel. 297/583–6000. $10. Mon.–Sat. 11–5.*

Built in 1962, **Beth Israel Synagogue** is the only Jewish house of worship on Aruba, and it strives to meet the needs of its Ashkenazi, Sephardic, European, North American, and South American worshipers. The island's Jewish community dates back to the opening of the oil refinery in the 1920s, when small congregations gathered in private homes in San Nicolas. The temple holds regular services on Friday at 8 PM and on Saturday at 8 AM; additional services are held on high holy days. Visitors are always welcome, although it's best to make an appointment to see the synagogue when there's not a service. A Judaica shop sells keepsakes, kosher dry goods, and kiddush wines. *Adrian Laclé Blvd. 2, tel. 297/582–3272. Free except high holy days.*

EASTERN ARUBA

In addition to the vast Arikok National Park, eastern Aruba is home to the island's second-largest city, San Nicolas, and several charming fishing villages and pristine beaches. Here you'll get a real sense of traditional island life.

A Good Tour

Take Route 1A to Route 4B and visit the Balashi Gold Smelter ruins and **FRENCHMAN'S PASS** ⑪. Return to 1A and continue your drive past Mangel Halto Beach to **SAVANETA** ⑫, a fishing village and one of several residential areas that has examples of typical Aruban homes. Follow 1A to **SAN NICOLAS** ⑬, where you can meander along the main promenade, pick up a few souvenirs, and grab a bite to eat. Heading out of town, continue on 1A until you hit a fork in the road; follow the signs toward **SEROE COLORADO** ⑭, with the nearby natural bridge and the Colorado Point Lighthouse. From here, follow the signs toward Rodgers Beach, just one of several area shores where you can kick back for a while. Nearby Baby Beach, with calm waters and beautiful white sand, is a favorite spot for snorkelers. To the north, on Route 7B, is Boca Grandi, a great windsurfing spot. Next is Grapefield Beach, a stretch of glistening white sand against a backdrop of cliffs and boulder formations. Shortly beyond it, on 7B, you'll come into **ARIKOK NATIONAL PARK** ⑮, where you can explore caves and tunnels, play on sand dunes, and tackle Mt. Yamanota, Aruba's highest elevation. Farther along 7B is Santa Cruz, where a wooden cross stands atop a hill to mark the spot where Christianity was introduced to the islanders. The same highway will bring you all the way into Oranjestad.

TIMING

You can follow the tour and see many of the sights in a half day, though it's easy to fill a full day if you spend time relaxing on a sandy beach or exploring the trails in Arikok National Park.

What to See

⑮ ARIKOK NATIONAL PARK. Nearly 20% of Aruba has been designated part of this national park, the keystone of the government's long-term ecotourism plan. Most of it sprawls across the interior, stretching to the north and encompassing a long strip of the windward shoreline. Within the confines of the park, near the island's center, is Mt. Arikok, the heart of a natural preserve that showcases the island's flora and fauna, the ruins of a gold-mining operation at Miralmar, and the remnants of Dutch peasant settlements at Masiduri. The 620-foot Mt. Yamanota, Aruba's highest peak, is also in the park.

Anyone looking for geological exotica should head for the park's caves, found on the northeastern coast. Baranca Sunu, the so-called Tunnel of Love, has a heart-shape entrance and naturally sculpted rocks farther inside that some say look like the Madonna, Abe Lincoln, and even a jaguar. Guadirikiri Cave and Fontein Cave are marked with ancient drawings (rangers are on hand to offer explanations), as both were used by indigenous people centuries ago. Bats are known to make appearances—don't worry, they won't bother you. Although you don't need a flashlight because the paths are well lighted, it's best to wear sneakers.

⑪ FRENCHMAN'S PASS. Overhanging trees and towering cacti border this luscious stretch of road. The pass is almost midway between Oranjestad and San Nicolas; follow L. G. Smith Boulevard past a shimmering vista of blue-green sea and turn off where you see the drive-in theater (a popular local hangout). Then proceed to the first intersection, turn right, and follow the curve to the right. Gold was discovered on Aruba in 1824, and near Frenchman's Pass are the massive concrete-and-limestone ruins of the **Balashi Gold Smelter,** a lovely place to picnic and listen to the chattering parakeets. A magnificent, gnarled divi-divi tree guards the entrance. The area now is home to Aruba's desalination plant, where all of the island's drinking water is purified.

Cunucu Houses

Pastel houses surrounded by cacti fences adorn Aruba's flat, rugged cunucu ("country" in Papiamento). The features of these traditional houses were developed in response to the environment. Early settlers discovered that slanting roofs allowed the heat to rise and that small windows helped to keep in the cool air. Among the earliest building materials was caliche, a durable calcium carbonate substance found in the island's southeastern hills. Many houses were also built using interlocking coral rocks that didn't require mortar (this technique is no longer used, thanks to cement and concrete). Contemporary design combines some of the basic principles of the earlier homes with touches of modernization: windows, though still narrow, have been elongated; roofs are constructed of bright tiles; pretty patios have been added; and doorways and balconies present an ornamental face to the world beyond.

13 SAN NICOLAS. During the heyday of the oil refineries, Aruba's oldest village was a bustling port; now its primary purpose is tourism. The institution in town is Charlie's Restaurant & Bar, a hangout for more than 50 years. Stop in for a drink and advice on what to see and do in this little town.

12 SAVANETA. The Dutch settled here after retaking the island in 1816, and it served as Aruba's first capital. Today it's a bustling fishing village with a 150-year-old *cas de torto* (mud hut), the oldest dwelling still standing on the island.

14 SEROE COLORADO. What was originally built as a community for oil workers is known for its intriguing 1939 chapel. The site is surreal, as organ-pipe cacti—nearly as tall as the refinery's belching smokestacks—form the backdrop for sedate whitewashed cottages. The real reason to come here is a second **natural bridge,** this one less well known. Keep bearing east past the community, continuing uphill until you run out of road. You can then hike down to the cathedral-like formation. It's not too strenuous, but watch your footing as you descend. Be sure to follow the white arrows painted on the rocks, as there are no other directional signs. Although this bridge isn't as spectacular as its more celebrated sibling, the raw elemental power of the sea that created it, replete with hissing blow holes, certainly is.

There's a traffic jam on L. G. Smith Boulevard—it's 11 PM on Friday and everyone is trying to get into Oranjestad. A cab pulls into the Havana Club parking lot, weaving through swarms of scantily clad women and casually dressed men. The pulse of Oreo, the island's most famous band, and an air of anticipation grip the night crawlers waiting to get in. Only when the oversize door swings open does the night really begin.

IN THIS CHAPTER

nightlife

THEY PUMP UP THE VOLUME at Aruba's resort bars when the sun sets. Unlike many other islands, nightlife here isn't confined to touristy folkloric shows. In addition to spending time in one of the many casinos, you can slowly savor a drink while the sun dips into the sea, dance to the beat of a local band, bar-hop in a colorful bus, or simply stroll along a deserted starlit beach.

HOW & WHEN

Arubans like to party—the more the merrier—and they usually start celebrating late in the evening. The action, mostly on weekends, doesn't pick up until around midnight. Casual yet trendy attire is the norm. Most bars don't have a cover charge, although most nightclubs do. Bigger clubs, such as Club Havana, may have lines on weekends, but they move quickly; use this time to start your socializing and you may just end up with a dance partner before you even set foot inside the door. Drink specials are available at some bars, and every establishment will gladly give you a free Balashi Cocktail (the local term for a glass of water). Both bars and clubs have either live bands or DJs, depending on the night.

No matter where you choose to party, be smart about getting back to your hotel. Drinking and driving, of course, is against the law. If you're within walking distance, go ahead and hoof it. Taxis are a good option if your hotel is farther away. The island is safe, and you'll probably wander with swarms of other visitors in town and along Palm Beach.

A Bartender's Life

For some people, tending bar is a job. But for Tariq Ohab, one of Aruba's most popular bartenders, it's a way of life. Born in Aruba, the islander has a passion for mixing cocktails and everything that goes along with it. "If I could have any bartending job in the world," he says, "I'd like to stay right here."

Ohab lived in the United States for about eight years, but eventually moved back to the island he loves—a fact that endears him to his local clients, who appreciate his knowledge of Aruban culture and tales of his travels. Ohab recalls swapping small-world stories with a couple from Spokane who were surprised to find he had once lived in Olympia. "I meet a lot of interesting people," he says. "Most of the people I meet are always ready to start a conversation and chat up a storm."

Café Bahia, a popular watering hole, has been Ohab's habitat for the past eight years. Although most of his clients are tourists trying to take their minds off their sunburns, plenty of celebrities drop by for a cold one. Baseball player Sidney Ponson, a native of Aruba, is a regular. One day O. J. Simpson himself paid a visit. "He ordered orange juice," says Ohab, "and that's no joke."

Ohab especially enjoys mixing up Café Bahia's specialty drinks. The best bang for the buck, according to Ohab, is called the Blackout. "It's the strongest drink we have," he says. "It's made with five shots: tequila, whiskey, amaretto, 151, and Southern Comfort. It's topped with cranberry juice; then we mix in some blue grenadine and it becomes black before your eyes." Served in a big glass, the concoction takes an average person about an hour to finish one off. Most customers, he adds, don't stop at just one.

...ay sound like Ohab's life is one big party, but he has a mellower side ...ll. On Sunday, his day off, you'll find him at home with his wife and ...s. "Since my job is so social, I go out every night of the week," he ... Sundays, it's all about the family."

SOURCES

For information on specific events check out the free magazines *Aruba Nights, Aruba Events, Aruba Experience,* and *Aruba Holiday,* all available at the airport and at hotels.

Bar-Hopping Buses

A couple of bus operators can turn a regular evening out on the town into a whirlwind tour of the island's hottest nightspots. One uniquely Aruban institution is a psychedelically painted '57 Chevy bus called the **KUKOO KUNUKU** (tel. 297/586–2010). Weeknights you'll find as many as 40 passengers traveling between half a dozen bars from sundown to around midnight. The $55 fee per passenger includes dinner, drinks, and picking you up (and pouring you out) at your hotel. Group and private charter rates are available. Needless to say, reservations are essential.

Bars

Catch a glimpse of the elaborate swimming pool with whirlpools, waterslides, and waterfalls from the Hyatt Regency Aruba Beach Resort & Casino's **ALFRESCO LOBBY BAR** (J. E. Irausquin Blvd. 85, Palm Beach, tel. 297/586–1234 Ext. 4265) while sipping a fine wine or a tropical cocktail. This is where guests gather to hear live music early in the evening and stop by for a nightcap after the casino closes. Many visitors, including those on party buses,

★ find their way to **CARLOS & CHARLIE'S** (Weststraat 3A, Oranjestad, tel. 297/582–0355), which may be why locals shy away from it. You'll find mixed drinks by the yard, Mexican fare, and American music from the '60s, '70s, and '80s.

In business since 1948, **CHETA'S BAR** (Paradera 119, Paradera, tel. 297/582–3689) is a real local joint that holds no more than four customers at a time. There aren't any bar stools, either, which is why most patrons gather out front. During the

Saturday-afternoon happy hour, people mingle in the street and lean on their cars while sipping a cold Balashi ($1.35) and munching on buns from Bright Bakery. No one even seems to mind that the bar's lack of a liquor license means it can't serve mixed drinks and that it must close by 9 PM (it opens at 8:30 AM, though). You can ★ watch the crowds from the terrace at **CHOOSE A NAME** (Havenstraat 36, Oranjestad, tel. 297/588–6200) or climb up on the bar for your karaoke debut. Bands perform several nights a week.

Drive into Seroe Colorado, on the far side of Coco's Beach, and you'll notice a two-level structure overlooking the crystal-clear bay. **COCO BEACH BAR & RESTAURANT** (Coco's Beach, Seroe Colorado, tel. 297/584–3434) is a popular spot for food and drinks any time of the day or night. For specialty drinks, try **IGUANA JOE'S** (Royal Plaza Mall, L. G. Smith Blvd. 94, Oranjestad, tel. 297/583–9373) The creative reptilian-theme decor is as colorful as the cocktails.

The beachfront **KOKOA** (Palm Beach, tel. 297/586–2050) is often full of beauties in skimpy bathing suits and windsurfers in baggy shorts. There's live local music Fridays and Sundays, with everything from reggae and salsa to pop. With painted parrots flocking on ★ the ceiling, **MAMBO JAMBO** (Royal Plaza Mall, L. G. Smith Blvd. 94, Oranjestad, tel. 297/583–3632) is daubed in sunset colors. Sip one of several concoctions sold nowhere else on the island, then browse for memorabilia at a shop next door.

With front-row seats to view the green flash—that ray of light that flicks through the sky as the sun sinks into the ocean—the **PALMS BAR** (Hyatt Regency Aruba Beach Resort & Casino, J. E. Irausquin Blvd. 85, Palm Beach, tel. 297/586–1234) is the perfect spot to enjoy the sunset. At La Cabana All Suite Beach Resort & Casino, the **SUNSET BAR** (J. E. Irausquin Blvd. 250, Eagle Beach, ¹. 297/587–9000) serves cocktails at the swim-up bar.

Brewing Up Something Special

There was a time when you could walk into any bar in Aruba and get a glass of water by asking for a Balashi Cocktail. (The name came from the fact that the desalination plant is in an area known as Balashi.) Since the creation of Balashi, the first locally brewed beer, such a drink order has a whole new meaning. Made by a German brewmaster in a state-of-the-art facility using only the finest hops and malt, Balashi is golden-colored pilsner.

Balashi is a source of local pride, even more so since it won the prestigious Monde Selection at an international competition in 2001. Visitors love it as well. "It's a big tourist thing," explains Gerben Tilma, general manager of the plant. "Everyone wants to know what the best local products are. Now we can tell them."

The **BALASHI BREWERY** (Balashi, tel. 297/585–4805) has free 30-minute tours that begin every half hour between 10 AM and 2 PM daily. There's also a souvenir shop, a café, and a 10,000-square-foot beer garden where you can enjoy a cold one.

Cruises

On the **SALTY DOG SUNSET CRUISE** (tel. 297/586–2010), aboard the 80-foot sailing vessel dubbed Mi Dushi, you can enjoy Caribbean snacks as you toast with champagne. The open-air bar makes a nice place to meet fellow travelers. Cruises depart Wednesdays and Fridays at 5 PM from the Aruba Grand Beach Resort Pier and return about 7 PM. The cost is $39 per person.

Don't be surprised if you're enjoying a romantic ocean-view dinner on Palm Beach and see a twinkle of lights on the horizon. It may be the **TATTOO** (tel. 297/586–2010), a catamaran that sails every night except Sunday from 8 PM to midnight. It has three decks for dancing (there are live bands and a DJ), dining, and stargazing. End the evening with the famous rope swing and waterslide. The cost is $49 per person.

Dance & Music Clubs

★ Popular with locals and tourists, **CAFÉ BAHIA** (Weststraat 7, Oranjestad, tel. 297/588–9982) draws a chic crowd every Friday for happy hour. Come for dinner and stick around for drinking and dancing as the music heats up. Tuesday nights, a band from one of the cruise ships plays local favorites. The newest hot spot is **CLUB HAVANA** (L. G. Smith Boulevard 2, Oranjestad, tel. 297/582–0152), where the Friday happy hour lasts until 2 AM. Two local bands jam live on Saturday from 10 PM to 4 AM.

The energy doesn't diminish until closing time at **TANTRA** (Royal Plaza Mall, L. G. Smith Blvd. 93, Oranjestad, tel. 297/583–8. ,2), where a young crowd lives for house and trance music. The dance floor and circular bar are always hopping. The cover charge is $5. **LA FIESTA** (Aventura Mall, Plaza Daniel Leo, Oranjestad, tel. 297/583–5896) attracts a casual yet classy crowd. A couple of laps around the wraparound terrace overlooking the main street gives night owls a chance to scope out the black-clad crowd. Inside, heavy red curtains add drama. Although there's no dance floor, a cool mix of music inspires patrons to bop at the bar.

Stop by the cozy **SIROCCO LOUNGE** (Wyndham Aruba Beach Resort & Casino, L. G. Smith Blvd. 77, Palm Beach, tel. 297/586–4466) for jazz every night except Sunday. For jazz and other types of music, try the cozy **GARUFA CIGAR & COCKTAIL LOUNGE** (Wilhelminastraat 63, Oranjestad, tel. 297/582–7205). It serves as a lounge for customers awaiting a table at the nearby El Gaucho Argentine Grill (you're issued a beeper so you know when your table is ready). While you wait, have a drink, enjoy some appetizers, and take in the leopard-print carpet and funky bar stools. The ambience may draw you back for an after-dinner cognac.

Local bands are always in the spotlight at the beach-side **GILLIGAN'S** (Radisson Aruba Caribbean Resort, J. E. Irausquin

Cool Concoctions

These drink recipes come from Aruban-born bartender Clive Van Der Linde.

THE WOW. Mix equal parts (2 ounces or so) of rum and vodka as well as triple sec, a splash of tequila, grenadine, coconut cream, and pineapple and orange juice. Quips Van Der Linde, "You won't taste the alcohol, but after two, you'll feel pretty good."

THE IGUANA. Mix equal parts of rum and vodka, and add either blue Curaçao or blue grenadine for color. Add crème de banana liqueur, coconut cream, and pineapple juice. Says Van Der Linde, "I learned this one more than 10 years ago on the first sailing boat I worked on. It was called the Balia, which means 'to dance.' "

THE CAPTAIN'S SPECIAL. Mix equal parts of rum and vodka, and add a splash of amaretto, crème de banana, and pineapple and orange juice. "It's really simple," says Van Der Linde. "Just blend with crushed ice and it's ready to drink."

Blvd. 81, Palm Beach, tel. 297/586–6555). You'll feel like you've been shipwrecked on an uncharted tropic isle as you sip cocktails at the bar. Musicians take to the stage every evening at **PATA PATA** (La Cabana All Suite Beach Resort & Casino, J. E. Irausquin Blvd. 250, Eagle Beach, tel. 297/587–9000). Live music every evening makes **PELICAN TERRACE** (Divi Aruba Beach Resort, J. E. Irausquin Blvd. 45 Manchebo Beach, tel. 297/582–3300) a popular nightspot. Sip creative cocktails, dance around the pool, and grab a late-night snack—perhaps a pizza that's piping hot from the wood-burning oven.

Local bands alternate sets at **RICK'S CAFÉ AMERICAN** (Wyndham Aruba Beach Resort & Casino, J. E. Irausquin Blvd. 77, Palm Beach, tel. 297/586–4466), a popular watering hole. The bar is inside the hotel's casino, so you can throw a quarter in

Temperature & Liquid Volume Conversion Chart

Temperature: Metric Conversions

*To change Centigrade or Celsius (C) to Fahrenheit (F),
multiply C by 1.8 and add 32. To change F to C, subtract 32
from F and multiply by .555.*

C°	F°	F°	C°
0	-17.8	60	15.5
10	-12.2	70	21.1
20	-6.7	80	26.6
30	-1.1	90	32.2
32	0	98.6	37.0
40	+4.4	100	37.7
50	10.0		

Liquid Volume: Liters/U.S. Gallons

*To change liters (L) to U.S. gallons (gal), multiply L by .264.
To change U.S. gal to L, multiply gal by 3.79.*

L to gal	gal to L
1 = .26	1 = 3.8
2 = .53	2 = 7.6
3 = .79	3 = 11.4
4 = 1.1	4 = 15.2
5 = 1.3	5 = 19.0
6 = 1.6	6 = 22.7
7 = 1.8	7 = 26.5
8 = 2.1	8 = 30.3

the slots on your way in—you just might win enough to cover your bar tab. At the **STELLARIS LOUNGE & LOBBY BAR** (Aruba Marriott Resort & Stellaris Casino, L. G. Smith Blvd. 101, Palm Beach, tel. 297/586–9000) local bands gets the party started about 9 PM and keep it going till at least 2 AM.

Movies

With six screens, **SEAPORT CINEMA** (Seaport Market Place, tel. 297/583–0318) has all the latest American movies. The earliest shows are around 4 PM; late shows start around 10:30 PM during the week and midnight on weekends. Ticket prices range from about $6 to $7.

Check out the not-so-silver screen under the stars at the **E. DE VEER DRIVE-IN THEATER** (Kibaima, tel. 297/585–8355). It will cost you about $3 to watch the English-language movies on this massive screen in a field near Balashi. Movies start at 8:30 PM. The drive-in can accommodate about 100 cars and has a snack bar.

Fun Without the Sun

At last count there were more than 50 theme nights offered during the course of a week. Each party features a buffet dinner, dancing, and entertainment (often of the limbo, steel-band, stilt-walking variety). The top groups tend to rotate among the resorts. For a complete list contact the Aruba Tourism Authority. One of the best theme parties is the **HAVANA TROPICAL** (Wyndham Aruba Beach Resort & Casino, J. E. Irausquin Blvd. 77, Palm Beach, tel. 297/586–4466), which rocks every night except Wednesday and Sunday.

It's Tuesday night at the Bon Bini Festival. Performers run onto the stage as steel-pan drummers pound out a heart-racing beat. The rhythm prompts a local dance troupe to converge on the scene; the audience is mesmerized by their traditional movements and colorful costumes. One observer, an island visitor, gets up and joins the dance. A local man with a bead of sweat on his brow flashes her a bright smile and says, "Hey, you ever seen this before? This is the good stuff."

IN THIS CHAPTER

the arts

PUERTO RICO HAS RICKY MARTIN, Jamaica has Bob Marley, and Aruba has . . . well, Aruba has a handful of stars who aren't quite as famous but are just as talented. Over the years, several local artists, including composer Julio Renado Euson (who once won a competition against Ricky Martin), choreographer Wilma Kuiperi, sculptor Ciro Abath, and visual artist Elvis Lopez, have gained international renown. Further, many Aruban musicians play more than one type of music (classical, jazz, soca, salsa, reggae, calypso, rap, pop), and many compose as well as perform.

The Union of Cultural Organizations is devoted to developing local arts while broadening its international appeal. UNOCA provides scholarships to help artists of all ages to participate in exhibitions, shows, and festivals. Although some internationally recognized stars have returned to Aruba to help promote the island's cultural growth, renowned conductor and pianist Eldin Juddan says the island needs to do more to promote local musicians. "There's a lot of talent, but professional guidance is needed to bring these talents and music to their potential. They [the professionals] can be instrumental in leading workshops, giving lectures, and organizing local performing- and visual-arts events. . . ."

The **CAS DI CULTURA** (Vondellaan 2, Oranjestad, tel. 297/582–1010), the island's cultural center, continuously hosts art exhibits, folkloric shows, dance performances, and concerts. Further, the island's many festivals showcase arts and culture. To find out what's going on, check out *Aruba Today*, the local newspaper, or *Calalou*, a Caribbean publication dedicated to the

In Tune with Jonathan Vieira

His parents were always traveling, so when musician Jonathan Vieira was growing up, he often stayed with his grandmother. He was fascinated with her old piano. He hit his first note when he was four, and has been playing ever since. The Aruba native, who taught himself to play, recorded an album called Two Generations with Padu del Caribe, one of the composers of the island's national anthem. Vieira speaks highly of his collaborator, calling him the "father of our culture."

"On Aruba, people need to have more of an awareness of cultural music," Vieira says. "The popular stuff catches on quick; we have to have a balance." Many of his own musical creations show his affinity for local rhythms, though he also is well versed in classical and contemporary music.

When he was about 14, a local promoter heard about his talents and invited him to open one of the concerts she was organizing. The reaction was positive, and for the first time Vieira realized he could use his talent to make some money—or at least pay his school expenses. At age 17, Vieira headed to the United States to continue his education. He is attending the Berkeley College of Business in New York City, where he is finishing a degree in information management systems. It's his third degree; the others are in film and video production and recording arts production. "On the island," says Vieira, "everyone knows me as a pianist."

Although his first love is music, 23-year-old Vieira has also been dabbling in film. "I have been doing a bit of acting recently to try it out," he says. In the meantime, Vieira is busy giving back to the island he calls home. He returns to Aruba in the summer to give chamber concerts at the Access, an art gallery and performance space in Oranjestad. He also invites other artists to join him in special holiday performances.

visual arts. You can also phone the national library, which has a bulletin board of events.

ART GALLERIES

★ **ACCESS GALLERY.** Showcasing new and established artists, this gallery is a major venue for Caribbean art. Located in the downtown shopping district, it is home to a thriving cultural scene that includes poetry readings, chamber music concerts, and screenings of feature films and documentaries. The owner, artist Landa Henriquez, is also a bolero singer. *Caya Betico Croes 16–18, Oranjestad, tel. 297/588–7837.*

GALERIA ETERNO. At this gallery you'll find local and international artists at work. Be sure to stop by for concerts by classical guitarists, and dance performances, visual-arts shows, and plays. *Emanstraat 92, Oranjestad, tel. 297/583–9484.*

GALERIA HARMONIA. The island's largest gallery has changing art exhibits as well as a permanent collection of works by local and international artists. *Zeppenfeldstraat 10, San Nicolas, tel. 297/584–2969.*

GASPARITO RESTAURANT & ART GALLERY. This exceptional dining spot features an ongoing exhibition of works by Aruban artists. Selected works are for sale. *Gasparito 3, Noord, tel. 297/586–7044.*

★ **INSIGHT.** This contemporary gallery hosts exhibitions of local and international artists. Don't expect to find the usual paintings of pastel-colored skies. Owner Alida Martinez, a Venezuelan-born artist, likes more avant-garde displays. Her own mixed-medium creations juxtapose erotic and religious themes. The space, which includes a studio, is a magnet for the island's art community. *Paradera Park 215, Paradera, tel. 297/582–0542.*

FESTIVALS

Annual Events

★ **THE DANDE STROLL.** New Year's Eve is a big deal in most places, but on Aruba, the fireworks that light up the sky at midnight are just the beginning. Celebrations continue throughout New Year's Day. Groups of musicians stroll from house to house, singing good-luck greetings for the New Year. A prize is awarded to the group with the best song, which is sung by islanders during the next 12 months. Dande, by the way, comes from the Papiamento word "dandara," which means "to have a good time."

INTERNATIONAL DANCE FESTIVAL ARUBA. Each October, dance companies from the Caribbean, the United States, and Europe participate in workshops, lectures, demonstrations, and exhibitions.

INTERNATIONAL THEATRE FESTIVAL ARUBA. Every other October, theater groups from around the world perform 45- to 70-minute shows at the Cas Di Cultura.

JAZZ AND LATIN MUSIC FESTIVAL. For a few nights each June, you can hear authentic jazz and Latin music performed at the outdoor venue next to the Renaissance Aruba Beach Resort at Seaport Village. There's a good deal of dancing in the aisles at this event. Tickets are available at the Aruba Tourism Authority office.

HI-WINDS PRO AM WINDSURFING COMPETITION. Windsurfers of all skill levels come from more than 30 different countries during June or July to put the island's ideal wind and surf conditions to use in competition off the beaches at Fisherman's Huts at Hadikurari.

NATIONAL ANTHEM & FLAG DAY. On this official holiday, held March 18, you can stop by Plaza Betico Croes in Oranjestad for folkloric presentations and other traditional festivities.

ST. JOHN'S DAY. Dera Gai, the annual "burying of the rooster" festival, is celebrated June 24, the Feast of St. John the Baptist.

Carnival

Aruba's biggest bash incorporates local traditions with those of Venezuela, Brazil, Holland, and North America. Here, Carnival consists of six weeks of jump-ups (traditional Caribbean street celebrations), competitions, parties, and colorful parades. The celebrations culminate with the Grand Parade held in Oranjestad on the Sunday before Ash Wednesday. It lasts for hours and turns the streets into one big stage. The two main events are the Grand Children's Parade, where kids dress in colorful costumes and decorate floats, and the Lightning Parade, consisting of miles of glittery floats and lavish costumes. Steel-pan and brass bands supply the music that inspires the crowds to dance. All events end on Shrove Tuesday: at midnight an effigy of King Momo (traditionally depicted as a fat man) is burned, indicating the end of joy and the beginning of Lenten penitence.

Festive songs, bright yellow-and-red costumes, and traditional dances mark this holiday dating from 1862. Today, the rooster—which symbolizes a successful harvest—has been replaced by a gourd.

Weekly Parties

BON BINI FESTIVAL. The name means "welcome" in Papiamento, which should give you an idea of what this festival is all about. The year-round folkloric event is held every Tuesday from 6:30 PM to 8:30 PM at Oranjestad's historic Fort Zoutman. In the inner courtyard you can check out the Antillean dancers in resplendent costumes, feel the rhythms of the steel drums, browse among the stands displaying local artwork, and partake of local food and drink. Admission is $3.

A visitor from the United States became frustrated when he couldn't get in touch with his family—either via the Internet or his long-distance phone service—from his hotel. Another hotelier overheard the visitor complain about the problem to a beach buddy. The hotelier immediately offered to let the visitor use the facilities at his hotel, handing over a key to the private computer room. And, of course, the hotelier also invited the visitor to join him for coffee.

IN THIS CHAPTER

where to stay

"CUIDA NOS TURISTA" ("TAKE CARE OF OUR TOURISTS") is the island's motto, and Arubans are taught the finer points of hospitality as soon as they learn to read and write. With such cordial hosts, it's hard to go wrong no matter which accommodation you choose.

Most hotels are west of Oranjestad, along L. G. Smith and J. E. Irausquin boulevards. Many are self-contained complexes, with restaurants, shops, casinos, water-sports centers, health clubs, and car-rental and travel desks. Room service, laundry and dry-cleaning services, in-room safes, minibars or refrigerators, and baby-sitting are standard at all but the smallest properties. Most places don't include meals in their rates. Still, you can shop around for good dining options, as hotel restaurants and clubs are open to all island guests.

Many people prefer to stay in time-shares, returning year after year and making the island a kind of home away from home. Some time-share patrons say they like the spacious, homey accommodations and the opportunity to prepare their own meals. Note that hotel-type amenities such as shampoo, hair dryers, and housekeeping service may not be offered in time-shares; if they are, they often cost extra. Note that both time-shares and hotels typically charge a combined total of 19% taxes and service charge on top of quoted rates, so be sure to ask about taxes before booking to avoid sticker-shock when you check out.

Plans are in the works to introduce a special program for frequent visitors to Aruba. This would include automatic check-in at the airport (sign in, get your key, and head right to your

Associations That Accommodate

The **ARUBA HOTEL & TOURISM ASSOCIATION** (tel. 297/582–2607) was established in 1965 to maintain high standards in the tourism industry. From its original seven hotels, the organization has grown into a powerhouse of more than 80 businesses, including restaurants, casinos, stores, tour operators, and airlines. The organization's $4 million annual budget, earmarked to promote Aruba as a travel destination, comes from the Aruba Tourism Authority and from private-sector partners. On the Aruba Tourism Web site at you can express opinions and register complaints. The organization is also involved in anti-litter efforts as part of the Aruba Limpi Committee.

Another association, the **ARUBA APARTMENT RESORT & SMALL HOTEL ASSOCIATION** (tel. 297/582–3289), represents smaller, less expensive hotels. Members are expected to meet certain standards of accommodation and service and still offer affordable rates (often as low as $65 per night).

hotel room). Check with your travel agent to see if the plan has taken effect and whether you qualify. There are, however, a few perks already in place for repeat island visitors: return for 10 consecutive years, and a picture taken of you and a tourist board representative will be published in a local paper. Come for 20 years in a row and you'll be named a goodwill ambassador to the island.

Prices

Hotel rates are high; to save money, take advantage of airline and hotel packages, or visit during the summer when rates are discounted by as much as 40%. If you're traveling with kids, ask about discounts; children often stay for free in their parents' room, though there are age cutoffs.

CATEGORY	HOTELS EP,BP, CP	HOTELS AI
$$$$	over $350	over $450
$$$	$250–$350	$350–$450
$$	$150–$250	$250–$350
$	$80–$150	$125–$250
¢	under $80	under $125

Prices are for two people in a standard double room in high season, excluding 8% taxes and 11% service charges.

$$$$ ★ ARUBA MARRIOTT RESORT & STELLARIS CASINO. You'll hear the sound of water everywhere at this high-rise hotel on Palm Beach, whether it's the beating of the surf below your generously sized balcony or the trickling of the waterfalls in the bright, air-conditioned lobby and around the tropically landscaped pool. Most of the Caribbean-style rooms have ocean views, as well as walk-in closets, hair dryers, and irons. Spacious suites have their own hot tubs. Tuscany offers superlative Italian cuisine, and Simply Fish serves dishes fresh from the sea. Express checkout is available. *L. G. Smith Blvd. 101, Palm Beach, tel. 297/586–9000 or 800/223–6388, fax 297/586–0649, www.marriott.com. 413 rooms, 20 suites. 4 restaurants, café, in-room data ports, in-room safes, minibars, cable TV with movies, in-room VCRs, 2 tennis courts, pool, fitness classes, health club, hair salon, massage, sauna, spa, beach, dive shop, windsurfing, boating, jet skiing, volleyball, 4 bars, casino, shops, concierge, Internet, meeting rooms, car rental. AE, D, DC, MC, V. EP.*

$$$$ ★ HYATT REGENCY ARUBA BEACH RESORT & CASINO. A honeymoon favorite, this resort resembles a Spanish palace, with art-deco flourishes and a multilevel pool with waterfalls, a two-story waterslide, and a lagoon stocked with tropical fish. Rooms have slim balconies, but lots of extras; those on the Regency Club floor have complimentary breakfast and concierge service. Relax on the beach, play tennis, or go horseback riding before an afternoon hydrotherapy treatment. Ruinas del Mar serves Continental fare, and Japengo is known for seafood with an Asian flair. The imaginative Camp Hyatt teaches kids Aruban-style

lodging

California Pt.

Mt. Altovista

Bushiribana

Palm Beach

16 – 27

14 15

29

28 Noord

Tanki Leedert

Paradera

Eagle Beach

8 – 13

Manchebo Beach

4 – 7

1 – 3

Santa

Druif Beach

Oranjestad

Druif
Bay

Surfside Beach

30

N

| 0 | | 4 miles |
| 0 | | 6 km |

Allegro Aruba
Resort &
Casino, 20

Amsterdam Manor
Beach Resort, 14

Aruba Beach
Club, 12

Aruba Grand
Beach Resort &
Casino, 22

Aruba Marriott
Resort & Stellaris
Casino, 18

Aruba Divi
Phoenix Beach
Resort, 25

Best Western
Manchebo Beach
Resort, 11

Best Western Talk
of the Town
Resort, 2

Boardwalk
Vacation
Retreat, 16

Brickell Bay Beach
Club, 27

Bucuti Beach
Resort, 10

La Cabana All
Suite Beach
Resort &
Casino, 15

Caribbean Palm
Village, 29

Casa Del Mar
Beach Resort, 3

Costa Linda Beach
Resort, 13

Divi Aruba Beach
Resort Mega All
Inclusive, 5

Divi Dutch
Village, 7

Divi Village, 6

Holiday Inn
Sunspree Aruba
Beach Resort &
Casino, **23**

Hyatt Regency
Aruba Beach
Resort &
Casino, **19**

Marriott's Aruba
Ocean Club, **17**

Mill Resort &
Suites, **28**

Paradise Beach
Villas, **8**

Playa Linda Beach
Resort, **26**

La Quinta Beach
Resort, **9**

Radisson Aruba
Resort &
Casino, **24**

Renaissance
Aruba
Resort & Casino, **1**

Tamarijn Aruba All
Inclusive Beach
Resort, **4**

Vistalmar, **30**

Wyndham Aruba
Beach Resort &
Casino, **21**

storytelling, Caribbean cooking, and arts and crafts. J. E. Irausquin Blvd. 85, Palm Beach, tel. 297/586–1234 or 800/554–9288, fax 297/586–5478, www.hyatt.com. 342 rooms, 18 suites. 5 restaurants, snack bar, room service, fans, in-room safes, minibars, cable TV with movies, 2 tennis courts, pool, health club, hair salon, 2 outdoor hot tubs, massage, sauna, spa, steam room, beach, dive shop, dock, snorkeling, windsurfing, boating, jet skiing, waterskiing, basketball, horseback riding, volleyball, 5 bars, casino, shops, babysitting, children's programs (ages 3–12), playground, concierge, Internet, business services, car rental, travel services. AE, D, DC, MC, V. EP.

$$$$ LA CABANA ALL SUITE BEACH RESORT & CASINO. Convenience is key at this self-contained resort across from Eagle Beach. About a third of the studios and one-bedroom suites have ocean views. All have kitchenettes, balconies, and hot tubs. Pricier villas are away from the main building. Planning to do your own cooking? You can order groceries online up to two days before your trip and have them delivered when you arrive. No need to bring a laptop; rent one for $25 a day, and get wireless Internet access for about $15 per day. The resort's supervised Club Cabana Nana program makes this a family favorite. J. E. Irausquin Blvd. 250, Eagle Beach, tel. 297/587–9000, 800/835–7193, fax 297/587–0844, www.lacabana.com. 803 suites. 3 restaurants, grocery, ice cream parlor, in-room safes, kitchenettes, microwaves, cable TV, 5 tennis courts, 3 pools, fitness classes, health club, 3 outdoor hot tubs, massage, sauna, spa, dive shop, basketball, racquetball, shuffleboard, squash, volleyball, 5 bars, video game room, shops, playground, Internet, meeting rooms. AE, D, DC, MC, V. EP.

$$$$ ★ MARRIOTT'S ARUBA OCEAN CLUB. First-rate amenities and lavishly decorated villas have made this time-share the talk of the island. Each one- and two-bedroom unit includes a kitchen and a balcony with a spectacular ocean view. The S-shape pool has a swim-up bar and waterfalls; there are four hot tubs built into the rocks above. You can access the facilities at the adjacent Aruba Marriott Resort & Stellaris Casino, including the spa, the fitness center, and the casino. An adjacent time-share property, Marriott's

Aruba Surf Club, is just as luxurious. *L. G. Smith Blvd. 99, Palm Beach, tel. 297/586–2641, fax 297/586–8000, www.marriott.com. 218 units. Restaurant, grocery, kitchenettes, microwaves, refrigerators, cable TV with movies, pool, spa, beach, dive shop, snorkeling, windsurfing, boating, jet skiing, shops, Internet, meeting rooms. AE, D, DC, MC, V. EP.*

$$$$ **RADISSON ARUBA RESORT & CASINO.** This resort—one of the
★ largest on the island—promises to pamper its guests. Rare birds greet you in the expansive lobby. Colonial Caribbean–style guest rooms (most with a view of the ocean or the garden) have mahogany four-poster beds and hand-beaded lamp shades. The designers thought of everything: blue accent lighting, wood furniture on the balconies, and plantation shutters. Unwind in the fitness center or spa, then enjoy a meal at one of the hotel's excellent restaurants. Try Gilligan's at the beach for simple fare, or the Sunset Grille for more elaborate dishes. *J. E. Irausquin Blvd. 81, Palm Beach, tel. 297/586–6555, fax 297/586–3260, www.radisson. com. 358 rooms, 32 suites. 4 restaurants, room service, in-room safes, minibars, cable TV with movies, golf privileges, 2 tennis courts, 2 pools, health club, spa, beach, dive shop, snorkeling, boating, jet skiing, 3 bars, video game room, babysitting, children's programs (ages 5–12), dry cleaning, laundry service, Internet, business services, convention center, meeting rooms. AE, D, DC, MC, V. BP.*

$$$–$$$$ **ALLEGRO ARUBA RESORT & CASINO.** Activity surrounds the cloverleaf-shape pool (with its waterfall and whirlpool tubs) at the heart of this resort. A popular place with tour groups, it always has something going on, from beer-drinking contests to bikini fashion shows. The tropical-theme rooms have white-tile bathrooms that are snug and balconies that are narrow step-outs, but better air-conditioning. The Kids' Club, which runs from 9 to 5 daily, keeps younger folks busy with a wide range of activities. *J. E. Irausquin Blvd. 83, Palm Beach, tel. 297/586–4500 or 800/448–8355, fax 297/586– 3191, www.occidentalhotels.com. 403 rooms, 14 suites. 3 restaurants, in- room safes, cable TV with movies, 2 tennis courts, pool, gym, 2 outdoor hot tubs, beach, snorkeling, boating, waterskiing, Ping-Pong, volleyball,*

3 bars, casino, dance club, shops, children's programs (ages 4–12), Internet, meeting rooms. AE, D, DC, MC, V. AI.

$$$–$$$$ COSTA LINDA BEACH RESORT. The name of this hotel, Spanish for "beautiful coast," speaks for itself. This paradise on earth is spread along a 600-foot stretch of pristine Eagle Beach. An inviting blue pool sits in the center of the manicured grounds. Pamper yourself with numerous amenities in the bright, spacious two-bedroom suites, including Roman tubs and balconies overlooking the crystalline sea. Larger units also have outdoor hot tubs and barbecue grills. There are lighted tennis courts on the premises, and scuba diving, snorkeling, and boating opportunities nearby. In the evening, take a stroll to the nearby Alhambra Casino. J. E. Irausquin Blvd. 59, Eagle Beach, tel. 297/583–8000, fax 297/583–6040, www.costalinda-aruba.com. 155 suites. 2 restaurants, kitchenettes, refrigerators, cable TV, 2 tennis courts, pool, wading pool, health club, 2 bars, shops, babysitting, children's programs (ages 5–12), dry cleaning, laundry facilities, Internet. AE, MC, V. EP.

$$$–$$$$ PLAYA LINDA BEACH RESORT. It's hard to separate fantasy from reality at this luscious pyramid-shaped resort. Set on a sandy white beach, its spacious studios and one- and two-bedroom suites are lavishly appointed. Frolic on the beach, dip in the free-form pool or one of the hot tubs, play a few games of tennis, or shop in the arcade. After preparing a meal in your fully equipped kitchen, enjoy the sunset from the large terrace. Other evening entertainment options include the free weekly cocktail party. Come morning, grab a quick bite at on-site Dushi Bagels. J. E. Irausquin Blvd. 87, Palm Beach, tel. 297/586–1000, fax 297/586–5210, www.playalinda.com. 204 units. Restaurant, in-room safes, kitchenettes, refrigerators, cable TV, putting green, 3 tennis courts, pool, health club, hot tub, beach, dive shop, windsurfing, boating, fishing, 2 bars, video game room, shops, babysitting, laundry facilities, Internet, meeting rooms. AE, D, DC, MC, V. CP.

$$–$$$$ ARUBA BEACH CLUB. Colonial charm and Dutch hospitality create an ambience that keeps families coming back year after year. All studios and one-bedroom units in this time-share property have bamboo furniture, satellite TVs, and balconies, sometimes with ocean views. There's plenty to do here, including yoga and language courses in Papiamento. The front desk can arrange for water sports and other activities. Kids enjoy the playground and their own pool. A shopping arcade is filled with boutiques, a frozen yogurt shop, and a cybercafe. If all this isn't enough, you can use the facilities at the adjoining Casa del Mar Beach Resort. J. E. Irausquin Blvd. 51–53, Punta Brabo Beach, tel. 297/582–3000, fax 297/582–6557, www.arubaonline.com/beachclub. 89 rooms, 42 suites. Restaurant, café, grocery, in-room safes, some kitchenettes, cable TV, 2 tennis courts, pool, wading pool, health club, hair salon, bar, video game room, shops, babysitting, children's programs (ages 3–12), playground, laundry service, Internet, meeting rooms, car rental, travel services. AE, D, DC, MC, V. EP.

$$–$$$$ **CASA DEL MAR BEACH RESORT.** This beachside resort offers two parts recreation, one part rest and relaxation. Deluxe accommodations are quite comfortable, with amenities such as balconies and fully equipped kitchens. Play tennis on one of four lighted courts, work out in the exercise room, arrange water sports at the activities desk, or kick back with a book from the library. Dine poolside at the Calypso restaurant. Kids enjoy the special programs offered weekdays from 10 to noon. L. G. Smith Blvd. 53, Manchebo Beach, tel. 297/582–3000 or 297/582–7000, fax 297/582–9044, www.casadelmar-aruba.com. 147 rooms. Restaurant, grocery, in-room safes, kitchenettes, refrigerators, cable TV with movies, 4 tennis courts, pool, wading pool, hair salon, hot tub, beach, bar, library, video game room, shops, children's programs (ages 4–10), laundry facilities, Internet, car rental, travel services. AE, D, DC, MC, V. EP.

$$–$$$$ **MILL RESORT & SUITES.** With clean geometric lines, the architecture of this small resort is striking. The resort's whitewashed, red-roof buildings surround its open-air common areas. Rooms are bright and attractive. Junior suites have sitting areas and kitchenettes. Smaller studios have full kitchens, tiny

baths, and no balconies. The beach is only a five-minute walk away; a morning coffee hour and a weekly scuba lesson are among the on-site amenities. At the Garden Café a special menu offers three courses at affordable prices. Board Fido or Fluffy overnight at the nearby vet. J. E. Irausquin Blvd. 330, Oranjestad, tel. 297/586–7700, fax 297/586–7271, www.millresort.com. 64 studios, 128 suites. Restaurant, grocery, in-room safes, kitchenettes, microwaves, cable TV, 2 tennis courts, 2 pools, wading pool, gym, massage, sauna, bar, laundry facilities, Internet, car rental, travel services. AE, D, DC, MC, V. EP.

$$$ ARUBA DIVI PHOENIX BEACH RESORT. A breathtaking location and a lively atmosphere make this hotel justifiably popular. Most of the studio and one- or two-bedroom units have balconies with ocean views. Tropical color schemes, wood furnishings, and lots of plants make you feel at home. Coffeemakers, microwaves, and hair dryers are among the thoughtful touches. Some rooms are wheelchair accessible. Sunset Beach Bistro serves breakfast, lunch, and dinner on the beach. Work it off in the state-of-the-art fitness center. In the evening, enjoy live entertainment or try your luck at the nearby Alhambra Casino. J. E. Irausquin Blvd. 75, Palm Beach, tel. 297/586–1170, fax 297/586–1165, www.arubaphoenix. com. 101 units. Restaurant, grocery, snack bar, fans, in-room safes, kitchenettes, microwaves, refrigerators, cable TV, in-room VCRs, golf privileges, pool, health club, hot tub, beach, snorkeling, boating, volleyball, 2 bars, shop, children's programs (ages 5–13), Internet, meeting rooms, travel services. AE, D, DC, MC, V. EP.

$$$ ARUBA GRAND BEACH RESORT & CASINO. Regulars return again and again to this beachfront resort for its relaxed atmosphere. The yellow-and-white building, with its distinctive jade-green roof, is accompanied by 55 thatch-roof beach huts. Large rooms and suites have such amenities as generous walk-in closets and balconies that overlook either the ocean, the pool, or the garden. The classic Seawatch restaurant serves international cuisine for breakfast, lunch, and dinner; the more casual Whale's Rib entices seafood lovers with fresh fish. Ask about packages; discounts are available for children under 12. J. E. Irausquin Blvd. 79, Palm Beach, tel. 297/586–3900 or 800/345–2782, fax 297/586–1941, www. arubagrand.com. 130 rooms, 41 suites. 2 restaurants, ice cream parlor, snack bar, room service, in-room safes, refrigerators, cable TV, 2 tennis courts, pool, wading pool, beach, dive shop, snorkeling, windsurfing, boating, waterskiing, volleyball, 3 bars, casino, shops, baby-sitting, dry cleaning, laundry service, concierge, meeting rooms. AE, D, DC, MC, V. EP.

$$$ WYNDHAM ARUBA BEACH RESORT & CASINO. From exciting windsurfing to sizzling nightlife, the Wyndham has something for everyone. Grand public spaces accommodate groups from North and South America, which make up most of the clientele. Rooms, a bit oddly configured, have mustard-color walls and handsome wood furniture. All have ocean-view balconies and amenities such as coffeemakers, minibars, and hair dryers. A "pool concierge" makes the rounds with magazines and CD players, and attendants spritz you with Evian, offer chilled towels, and serve frozen drinks. Treat yourself to a massage at the spa, just steps from the sand. End the evening with a cocktail at the Sirocco Lounge. J. E. Irausquin Blvd. 77, Palm Beach, tel. 297/586–4466 or 800/996–3426, fax 297/ 586–8217, www.wyndham.com. 481 rooms, 81 suites. 6 restaurants, in-room safes, minibars, cable TV, tennis court, pool, wading pool, 2 outdoor hot tubs, hair salon, massage, sauna, steam room, beach, dive shop, snorkeling, windsurfing, boating, jet skiing, parasailing, waterskiing, 5 bars, casino, video game room, shops, concierge, Internet, convention center. AE, D, DC, MC, V. EP.

$$–$$$ BOARDWALK VACATION RETREAT. The owners describe this small hotel as offering "far-from-it-all tranquillity with close-to-it-all convenience." A stay here puts you only a few yards from the beach and water sports and within walking distance of casinos. The suites are in casitas enveloped by gardens where hummingbirds and butterflies dart among the exotic palm trees. The rooms have comfortable rattan furnishings, large living rooms and kitchens, and patios with barbecue grills and hammocks. Housekeeping is provided every other day, and laundry service is available.

Bakval 20, Palm Beach, tel. 297/586–6654, fax 297/586–1836, *www.theboardwalk-aruba.com.* 13 units. *Grocery, kitchenettes, microwaves, refrigerators, cable TV, in-room VCRs, pool, wading pool, hot tub, babysitting. AE, MC, V. EP.*

$$–$$$ BUCUTI BEACH RESORT. On the widest, most secluded section of Eagle Beach, this European-style resort is a cut above the rest. Hacienda-style buildings house sunny rooms with cherrywood furnishings, sparkling tile floors, and ocean-view terraces. Extras include coffeemakers, microwaves, and hair dryers. The oceanfront Tara Wing, with its chic rooms and soothing spa, opened in 2004. Work out in the open-air fitness pavilion surrounded by lush gardens. Revel in rare 24-hour Internet access and wireless broadband connection throughout the resort—even on the beach. The hotel consistently wins awards for being environmentally conscientious. *L. G. Smith Blvd. 55-B, Eagle Beach, tel. 297/583–1100, fax 297/582–5272, www.bucuti.com. 97 rooms, 39 suites, 12 huts. Restaurant, grocery, fans, in-room safes, minibars, microwaves, refrigerators, cable TV, pool, beach, bicycles, 2 bars, shop, laundry facilities, Internet, business services, travel services. AE, D, DC, MC, V. CP.*

$$–$$$ DIVI ARUBA BEACH RESORT MEGA ALL INCLUSIVE. At this Mediterranean-style resort, you have your choice of standard rooms, beachfront lanais, or casitas that overlook courtyards and are often only steps from the beach. The mint-and-jade color scheme and white-tile floors are soothing. Make your own strawberry daiquiri and order piping hot pizzas at the poolside Pelican Bar. In addition to the many on-site facilities, you can also use those at the adjacent Tamarijn Aruba All Inclusive Beach Resort. Despite the "mega-all-inclusive" label, getting your laundry done, indulging in a spa treatment, or hiring a babysitter costs extra. *L. G. Smith Blvd. 93, Manchebo Beach, tel. 297/582–3300 or 800/554–2008, fax 297/583–1940, www.diviaruba.com. 203 rooms. 5 restaurants, fans, refrigerators, cable TV, golf privileges, tennis court, 2 pools, gym, hair salon, outdoor hot tub, beach, dive shop, snorkeling, windsurfing, boating, waterskiing, bicycles, shuffleboard, volleyball, 3 bars, shops, babysitting, laundry service, Internet. AE, D, DC, MC, V. AI.*

$$–$$$ PARADISE BEACH VILLAS. This low-rise resort attracts many perennial visitors—the sophisticated set that returns year after year is generally over 30. The suites (some accessible to people with disabilities) have spacious bedrooms and fully equipped kitchens. Some also have hot tubs and large balconies with ocean views. Splash around at one of the two large pools or mellow out in one of the outdoor whirlpools. Head to the rooftop deck for a margarita at the Star Gazer bar. For more action, try water sports— from banana-boat rides to jet-skiing jaunts—at the nearby beach. On-site conveniences include a drugstore and a small grocery. L. G. Smith Blvd., Eagle Beach, tel. 297/587–4000, fax 297/587–0071, www.paradisebeachvillas.com. 80 units. 2 restaurants, grocery, kitchenettes, microwaves, refrigerators, 2 pools, gym, 2 hot tubs, beach, 2 bars, shops, Internet, meeting room. AE, D, MC, V. EP.

$$–$$$ RENAISSANCE ARUBA BEACH RESORT & CASINO. If you want to be in the thick of things, this lively complex is surrounded by shops, restaurants, and casinos. It's a top choice for singles, yet also has plenty of activities for families. The newer building, near a private beach, has roomy suites with balconies and kitchenettes. The original high-rise has compact, attractive rooms with step-out balconies; choose the quieter garden-view rooms. In the lobby, connected to the Seaport Mall, you can board a skiff for a day trip to a 40-acre private island. Later, wind down at the spa. The gourmet restaurant, L'Escale, is one of Aruba's best. L. G. Smith Blvd. 82, Oranjestad, tel. 297/583–6000 or 800/766–3782, fax 297/582–5317, www.arubarenaissance.com. 560 rooms, 15 suites. 5 restaurants, room service, kitchenettes, minibars, some microwaves, cable TV with movies, golf privileges, tennis court, 3 pools, 2 gyms, massage, spa, beach, dive shop, snorkeling, marina, fishing, volleyball, 5 bars, 2 casinos, nightclub, video game room, shops, children's programs (ages 5–12), playground, laundry facilities, concierge, Internet, convention center, meeting rooms, no-smoking rooms. AE, D, DC, MC, V. EP.

$$–$$$ TAMARIJN ARUBA ALL INCLUSIVE BEACH RESORT. Low-rise buildings stretch along the shore at this all-inclusive resort catering to couples and families. The spacious oceanfront rooms, filled with pale wood furnishings, have private balconies. The rate covers food, beverages, entertainment, an array of activities, and even tickets to the weekly Bon Bini Festival. A bar at one end of the property serves food and drinks as a convenience for guests more removed from the main restaurants. A free shuttle runs to the Alhambra Casino until 3 AM. J. E. Irausquin Blvd. 41, Punta Brabo Beach, tel. 297/582–4150 or 800/554–2008, fax 297/525–5203, www.tamarijnaruba.com. 236 rooms. 3 restaurants, snack bar, fans, cable TV, golf privileges, 2 tennis courts, 2 pools, health club, beach, snorkeling, windsurfing, boating, waterskiing, fishing, bicycles, Ping-Pong, shuffleboard, volleyball, 2 bars, shops, Internet, meeting rooms, car rental. AE, D, DC, MC, V. AI.

$–$$$ HOLIDAY INN SUNSPREE ARUBA BEACH RESORT & CASINO. Three seven-story buildings filled with spacious rooms are set along a sugary, palm-dotted shore. The pool's cascades and sundeck draw as large a crowd as the beach, where you can enjoy the Wednesday evening cocktail party. Enjoy live entertainment as you try your luck at the casino, or savor fresh fish at the oceanfront Sea Breeze Grill. Work out at the fitness center and get massaged and wrapped at the spa. The resort's free program for kids is a boon for families. J. E. Irausquin Blvd. 230, Palm Beach, tel. 297/586–3600, 800/934–6750, fax 297/586–5165, www.holidayinn-aruba.com. 600 rooms, 7 suites. 4 restaurants, refrigerators, cable TV with movies, 4 tennis courts, 2 pools, gym, hair salon, massage, beach, dive shop, dock, snorkeling, windsurfing, boating, waterskiing, basketball, Ping-Pong, volleyball, 3 bars, casino, video game room, shops, children's programs (ages 5–12), concierge, Internet, meeting rooms. AE, D, DC, MC, V. EP.

$$ AMSTERDAM MANOR BEACH RESORT. This mustard-yellow hotel—all gables and turrets—looks like part of a Dutch colonial village. It's a cozy enclave surrounding a pool with a waterfall, with Eagle Beach just across the street. Rooms are furnished in either Dutch modern or provincial style and range from small studios—some with ocean-view balconies—to two-bedroom suites with peaked ceilings, full kitchens, and whirlpool tubs. Children under

Rest Easy

Even the softest of sheets can feel scratchy against sunburned skin. Before bed, try a local product made with the aloe vera plant—an Aruban treasure that's been cultivated here since the 1840s. The gel from inside the plant's fibrous water-retaining leaves is the key skin-moisturizing ingredient in Burn Balm, made by **ARUBA ALOE BALM** *(tel. 297/588–3222, 800/952–7822, www. arubaaloe.com). Besides this great after-sun soother, the company puts aloe in everything from lipstick to soap to hair spray.*

If a pre-bed application of an aloe product doesn't soothe your sun-kissed skin, perhaps a local sleeplessness remedy will. The rest of the world may resort to counting sheep, but Aruban insomniacs turn to basil. Babies who can't settle in are given an herbal tea made from the tops of the white basil plant, which grows everywhere on the island. If your valerian root doesn't do the trick, a more potent version of this tea just might.

12 stay free with their parents. Free diving lessons are available. J. E. Irausquin Blvd. 252, Eagle Beach, tel. 297/587–1492 or 800/932–6509, fax 297/587–1463, www.amsterdammanor.com. 72 units. Restaurant, fans, in-room safes, kitchenettes, microwaves, cable TV with movies, pool, wading pool, snorkeling, bar, playground, laundry facilities, Internet, car rental, some pets allowed. AE, D, DC, MC, V. EP.

$$ BEST WESTERN MANCHEBO BEACH RESORT. Set amid 100 acres of gardens, this resort feels miles away from it all; in reality it's just five minutes from town and across from a complex with shops, restaurants, and a casino. Rooms are decorated with blond-wood furnishings and bright floral fabrics and are equipped with such amenities as coffeemakers. The all-inclusive package treats you to a-la-carte breakfast at the poolside Garden Terrace, lunch at the Pega Pega restaurant, dinner at the French Steakhouse (famous for Argentine-style steaks), and unlimited house drinks at the bar.

A pavilion on one of the prettiest stretches of Eagle Beach is the site of many weddings. *J. E. Irausquin Blvd. 55, Eagle Beach, tel. 297/582–3444 or 800/223–1108, fax 297/583–2446, www.manchebo.com. 71 rooms. 2 restaurants, snack bar, fans, in-room safes, refrigerators, cable TV, pool, beach, snorkeling, 2 bars, shops, Internet, car rental. AE, D, DC, MC, V. EP.*

$$ BRICKELL BAY BEACH CLUB. Once overshadowed by the high-rises along Palm Beach, Brickell Bay now has an enviable location in the heart of a booming restaurant district. The moderate prices mean you sample every enticing entrée. There's no grand ocean view, but the simple and sunny rooms and the sparkling pool keep guests content. There's a bus stop close to the hotel, but the convenient golf carts that run to and from the beach can't be beat. The owner also runs the Excelsior Casino, so you'll get $5 at check-in to start you out at the tables. *J. E. Irausquin Blvd. 370, Palm Beach, tel. 297/586–0900, fax 297/586–4957, www.brickellbayaruba.com. 101 rooms. Coffee shop, grocery, cable TV, pool, video game room, Internet, meeting rooms, some pets allowed. AE, D, DC, MC, V. EP.*

$$ CARIBBEAN PALM VILLAGE. Lush gardens lend an air of tranquillity to this tile-roof resort not far from Palm Beach. Some of the one- and two-bedroom accommodations have fully equipped kitchens; all have private balconies. Eat breakfast or lunch at the pool bar, then swim a few laps or serve up a few aces on the tennis court. The hotel, a short walk from restaurants, casinos, and nightclubs, generally attracts people over 30. Although Eagle Beach is only a 10-minute walk from the resort, free shuttle buses depart for the sand weekdays at 9:25 AM and 2:25 PM and return at 12:30 PM and 4 PM. *Palm Beach Rd., Noord 43E, Noord, tel. 297/586–2700, fax 297/586–2380. 170 rooms. Restaurant, fans, some kitchenettes, microwaves, refrigerators, cable TV, tennis court, 2 pools, hot tub, bar, babysitting, car rental. AE, DC, MC, V. EP.*

$$ DIVI DUTCH VILLAGE. Enjoy old-world ambience while basking in new-world comforts at this oceanfront time-share set around a pair of free-form freshwater pools. Many handcrafted accents adorn the Spanish-style rooms, which have kitchens and hot tubs. Larger rooms also have private patios or balconies. You can participate in various outdoor activities and dine in one of several restaurants at the adjoining resorts. The nearby Alhambra Casino provides plenty of opportunities for shopping and gambling. Kids under 15 stay free. *J. E. Irausquin Blvd. 47, Oranjestad, tel. 297/ 583–5000 or 800/367–3484, fax 297/582–0501, www.diviresorts.com. 97 units. Kitchenettes, microwaves, refrigerators, cable TV, golf privileges, 2 pools, hot tubs, beach, Internet, some pets allowed. AE, D, DC, MC, V. EP.*

$$ DIVI VILLAGE GOLF & BEACH RESORT. A tropical feel pervades this self-contained time-share resort across the street from the beach. Accommodations run the gamut from efficiencies to suites to penthouses. All have such amenities as full kitchens, and many have balconies or terraces with views of the golf course or the ocean. Enjoy tennis and water sports, then head off to the nearby shops, restaurants, and nightclubs. The Alhambra Casino is a short walk. At press time, 240 more rooms were on the way. *J. E. Irausquin Blvd. 47, Oranjestad, tel. 297/583–5000 or 800/367–3484, fax 297/582– 0501, www.diviresorts.com. 153 units. Restaurant, kitchens, microwaves, refrigerators, cable TV, golf privileges, tennis court, bar. AE, DC, MC, V. EP.*

$$ LA QUINTA BEACH RESORT. A relaxed atmosphere makes this time-share resort appealing. One-, two-, and three-bedroom apartments have living-dining areas and kitchenettes. All except the very smallest have balconies with garden or ocean views, and many have their own hot tubs. Daily housekeeping is a real perk. The resort is adjacent to the Alhambra Casino and across the street from the beach. *L. G. Smith Blvd. 228, Eagle Beach, tel. 297/ 587–5010, fax 297/587–6263, www.webnova.com/laquinta. 54 units. Kitchenettes, microwaves, refrigerators, cable TV, 2 pools, bar, baby-sitting, laundry service, Internet, car rental. AE, D, MC, V. EP.*

$ BEST WESTERN TALK OF THE TOWN RESORT. For simple, moderately priced accommodations convenient to all that downtown has to offer, look no further. A palm-lined courtyard,

An Aruban Lullaby

This quirky little lullaby has been passed down from generation to generatio on Aruba. Once they hear it, children generally go right to sleep—out of fear

PAPIAMENTO:

Riba Cero di Biento
Ting Un Baca Malucu,
Muchanan Cu Ta Yora
Baca Ta Bin Come Nan.

ENGLISH:

On the windy mountain
There is a cranky cow,
And when children cry
The cow comes and eats them.

complete with a pool, hot tub, and open-air bar and restaurant, is the centerpiece of this resort, which attracts a lot of students. The brightly decorated rooms all have kitchenettes; some are accessible to people with disabilities. The property is just outside of town, but the friendly staff is happy to point you in the right direction. *L. G. Smith Blvd. 2, Oranjestad, tel. 297/582–3380, fax 297/ 583–2446, www.talkofthetownaruba.com. 63 rooms. Restaurant, in-room safes, kitchenettes, microwaves, refrigerators, cable TV, pool, hot tub, bar, laundry service, meeting rooms. AE, MC, V. EP.*

$ VISTALMAR. When Alby and Katy Yarzagary met at a Christmas party more than 20 years ago, they clicked. After they wed, they converted this property across the street from the fishing pier into a homey inn. Simply furnished one-bedroom apartments each have a full kitchen, a living-dining area, and a sunny porch. The

Yarzagarys provide snorkeling gear and stock the refrigerators with breakfast fixings. There's no beach at this spot south of town, but the sea is just across the street. The major drawback is the distance from shopping and dining options, but you can ride the bus that departs from the hotel five times daily. *Bucutiweg 28, Oranjestad, tel. 297/582–8579, fax 297/582–2200, www.arubavistalmar.com. 8 rooms. Kitchenettes, microwaves, cable TV with movies, laundry facilities, car rental. D. CP.*

practical information

Addresses

"Informal" might best describe Aruban addresses. Sometimes the street designation is in English (as in J. E. Irausquin Blvd.), other times in Dutch (as in Wilhelminastraat); sometimes it's not specified whether something is a boulevard or a *straat* (street) at all. Street numbers follow street names, and postal codes aren't used at all. In rural areas, you might have to ask a local for directions—and be prepared for such instructions as "Take a right at the market, then a left where you see the big divi-divi tree."

Air Travel

There are nonstop flights to Aruba from Charlotte, Chicago (seasonal service), Houston, Miami, Newark, New York–JFK, and Philadelphia. Canadian travelers must connect to a U.S. flight.

BOOKING YOUR FLIGHT

When you book **look for nonstop flights** and **remember that "direct" flights stop at least once.** Try to avoid connecting flights, which require a change of plane. Two airlines may operate a connecting flight jointly, so ask if your airline operates every segment of the trip; you may find that the carrier you prefer flies you only part of the way. To find more booking tips and to check prices and make online flight reservations, log on to www.fodors.com.

CARRIERS

American Airlines offers daily nonstop service from Miami, New York, and San Juan, and weekly service from Boston; American Eagle also flies from San Juan daily. Continental Airlines has nonstop service daily from Houston and Newark. Delta flies nonstop daily from Atlanta and weekly from New York's JFK. KLM offers regular service from Amsterdam. United flies weekly from Chicago and seasonally from Dulles in Washington, D.C. US Airways flies daily from Charlotte and Philadelphia.

Air DCA flies from Miami. The airline also has connecting flights to Caracas, Bonaire, Curaçao, St. Maarten, and other islands.

Check with the airlines during high travel season for flight and route additions, as service is sometimes increased in response to a rise in tourism.

➤AIRLINES & CONTACTS: **Air DCA** (tel. 297/582–1919 or 297/583–8080 on Aruba, 800/327–7230 in North America, www.flydce.com). **American/American Eagle** (tel. 297/582–2700 on Aruba, 800/433–7300 in North America, www.aa.com). **Continental** (tel. 297/588–0044 on Aruba, 800/525–0280 in North America, www.continental.com). **Delta** (tel. 297/588–0044 on Aruba, 800/241–4141 in North America, www.delta.com). **KLM** (tel. 297/582–3546 on Aruba, 31/20–4–747–747 in Amsterdam, www.klm.com in the Netherlands). **United Airlines** (tel. 297/588–6544 on Aruba, 800/538–2929 in North America, www.united.com). **US Airways** (tel. 297/800–1580 on Aruba, 800/428–4322 in North America, www.usairways.com).

CHECK-IN & BOARDING

Checking in, paying departure taxes (if they aren't included in your ticket), clearing security, and boarding can take time on Aruba. Because security has gotten tighter, **get to the airport at least three hours ahead of time.** You may be randomly selected for inspection of your carry-on baggage at the gate. Regulations prohibit certain items to be packed in your carry-on luggage, including batteries, cameras, cell phones, matches, lighters, and handheld radios. Check with your hotel concierge before packing to return home.

Assuming that not everyone with a ticket will show up, airlines routinely overbook planes. When everyone does, airlines ask for volunteers to give up their seats. In return, these volunteers usually get a certificate for a free flight and are rebooked on the next flight out. If there are not enough volunteers, the airline must choose who will be denied boarding. The first to get bumped are passengers who checked in late and those flying on discounted tickets, so **get to the gate and check in as early as possib**' especially during peak periods.

Always **bring a government-issued photo I.D. to the airport;** even when it's not required, a passport is best.

FLYING TIMES

Aruba is 2½ hours from Miami, 4½ hours from New York, and 9½ hours from Amsterdam. The flight from New York to San Juan, Puerto Rico, takes 3½ hours; from Miami to San Juan it's 1½ hours; and from San Juan to Aruba it's just over an hour. Shorter still is the ¼- to ½-hour hop (depending on whether you take a prop or a jet plane) from Curaçao to Aruba.

RECONFIRMING

Check the status of your flight before you leave for the airport. You can do this on your carrier's Web site, by linking to a flight-status checker (many Web booking services offer these), or by calling your carrier or travel agent. Always confirm international flights at least 72 hours ahead of the scheduled departure time.

Be sure to **reconfirm your flights on smaller carriers.** You may be transferred to another flight if there are not enough passengers, or your plane may make unscheduled stops to pick up more clients or cargo. It's all part of the excitement—and unpredictability—of Caribbean travel. In addition, regional carriers usually have weight restrictions. Make sure to **travel light** or you could be subject to outrageous surcharges or be forced to put very large or heavy luggage on another flight. For any further information on entry requirements to Aruba, visit www.aruba.com.

Airport & Transfers

AIRPORT

Aruba's Aeropuerto Internacional Reina Beatrix (Queen Beatrix International Airport), near the island's south coast, is a modern, passenger-friendly facility. Renovations in 2001 brought new concession areas, business lounges, escalators, elevators, rest rooms, covered walkways, and baggage claim areas.

➤**AIRPORT INFORMATION: Aeropuerto Internacional Reina Beatrix** (tel. 297/582–4800).

TRANSFERS

A taxi from the airport to most hotels takes about 20 minutes. It will cost about $16 to get to the hotels along Eagle Beach, $18 to the high-rise hotels on Palm Beach, and $9 to the hotels downtown. You'll find a taxi stand right outside the baggage claim area.

Business Hours

Bank hours are weekdays 8:15–5:45, with some branches closing for lunch from noon to 1. The Caribbean Mercantile Bank at the airport is open Saturday 9–4 and Sunday 9–1. The central post office in Oranjestad, catercorner from the San Francisco Church, is open weekdays 7:30–noon and 1–4:30. Shops are generally open Monday–Saturday 8:30–6. Some stores close for lunch from noon to 2. Many shops also open when cruise ships are in port on Sunday and holidays.

Bus Travel

Each day, from 6 AM to midnight, buses make hourly trips between the beach hotels and downtown Oranjestad. The one-way fare is $1.15, and the round-trip fare is $2. Exact change is preferred. Buses also run down the coast from Oranjestad to San Nicolas for the same fare. Contact the Aruba Tourism Authority for schedules. Buses run from the airport terminal to hotels every 15 minutes during the day until 8 PM, and once an hour from 8:40 PM to 12:40 AM.

Car Rental

You'll need a valid driver's license to rent a car, and you must meet the minimum age requirements of each rental service (Budget, for example, requires drivers to be over 25; Avis, over 23; and Hertz, over 21). A signed credit-card slip or a cash deposit of $500 is required. Rates for unlimited mileage are between $35 and $65 a day, with local agencies generally offering lower rates. Insurance is available starting at about $10 per day. Try to make reservations before arriving, and opt for a four-wheel-drive vehicle if you plan to explore the island.

➤AGENCIES: **Avis** (Kolibristraat 14, Oranjestad, tel. 297/582–8787, www.avis.com; Airport, tel. 297/582–5496). **Budget** (Kolibristraat 1, Oranjestad, tel. 297/582–8600 or 800/472–3325, www.budget.com). **Dollar** (Grendeaweg 15, Oranjestad, tel. 297/582–2783, www.dollar.com; Airport, tel. 297/582–5651; Manchebo Beach Resort, J. E. Irausquin Blvd. 55, tel. 297/582–6696). **Economy** (Kolibristraat 5, tel. 297/582–5176, www.economyaruba.com). **Hedwina Car Rental** (Bubali 93A, Noord, tel. 297/587–6442; Airport, tel. 297/583–0880). **Hertz** (Sabana Blanco 35, near the airport, tel. 297/582–1845, www.hertz.com; Airport, tel. 297/582–9112). **National** (Tanki Leendert 170, Noord, tel. 297/587–1967, www.nationalcar.com; Airport, tel. 297/582–5451). **Thrifty** (Balashi 65, Santa Cruz, tel. 297/585–5300, www.thrifty.com; Airport, tel. 297/583–5335).

Car Travel

Most of Aruba's major attractions are fairly easy to find; others you'll happen upon only by sheer luck (or with an Aruban friend). Aside from the major highways, the island's winding roads are poorly marked (although the situation is slowly improving). International traffic signs and Dutch-style traffic signals (with an extra light for a turning lane) can be misleading if you're not used to them; use extreme caution, especially at intersections, until you grasp the rules of the road. Speed limits are rarely posted but are usually 80 kph (50 mph) in the countryside.

GASOLINE

Gas prices average a little less than $1 a liter (roughly ⅓ gallon), which is reasonable by Caribbean standards. Stations are plentiful in and near Oranjestad, San Nicolas, and Santa Cruz and near the major high-rise hotels on the western coast. All take cash, and most take major credit cards.

PARKING

There aren't any parking meters in downtown Oranjestad, and finding an open spot is very difficult. Try the lot on Calle G. F. Betico Croes across from the First National Bank, the one on Havenstraat near the Chez Matilde restaurant, or the one on Emanstraat near the water tower. Rates average $1.25 an hour, but some charge almost twice that.

Children on Aruba

Kids of all ages love the beach, which means they love Aruba. Resorts are increasingly sensitive to families' needs, and many now have playgrounds and extensive children's programs, and can arrange for babysitters. On sightseeing days try to **include some activities that will also interest your kids.** If you are renting a car, don't forget to **arrange for a car seat** when you reserve. For general advice about traveling with children, consult *Fodor's FYI: Travel with Your Baby* (available in bookstores everywhere).

FLYING

If your children are two or older, **ask about children's airfares.** As a general rule, infants under two not occupying a seat fly at greatly reduced fares or even for free. When booking, **confirm carry-on allowances** if you're traveling with infants. In general, for babies charged 10% of the adult fare you are allowed one carry-on bag and a collapsible stroller; if the flight is full, the stroller may have to be checked or you may be limited to less.

Experts agree that it's a good idea to use safety seats aloft for children weighing less than 40 pounds. Airlines set their own policies: U.S. carriers usually require that the child be ticketed, even if he or she is young enough to ride free, since the seats must be strapped into regular seats. Do **check your airline's policy about using safety seats during takeoff and landing.** Safety seats are not allowed everywhere in the plane, so get your seat assignments as early as possible.

When reserving, **request children's meals or a freestanding bassinet** (not available at all airlines) if you need them. But note that bulkhead seats, where you must sit to use the bassinet, may lack an overhead bin or storage space on the floor.

FOOD

Even if your youngsters are picky eaters, meals in the Caribbean shouldn't be a problem. Baby food is easy to find, and hamburgers and hot dogs are available at many resorts. Restaurant menus offer pasta, pizza, sandwiches, and ice cream. Supermarkets have cereal, snacks, and other packaged goods you'll recognize from home. At outdoor markets a few dollars will buy you enough bananas, mangoes, and other fresh fruit to last your entire vacation.

LODGING

Children are welcome in most Aruban resorts, and those under 12 or 16 can often stay free in their parents' room. Be sure to **find out the cutoff age for children's discounts** when booking.

PRECAUTIONS

To avoid immigration problems if your child has a different last name, **bring identification that clarifies the family relationship** (e.g., a birth certificate identifying the parent or a joint passport).

SUPPLIES & EQUIPMENT

Suites at many resorts and even small hotels have sofa beds suitable for children sharing a parent's room. High chairs and cribs are also generally available. Supermarkets sell common brands of disposable diapers, baby food, and other necessities. Bookstores and souvenir shops have activity books and toys that kids will enjoy on vacation and back at home.

Cruise Travel

Cruising is a relaxed and convenient way to tour this beautiful part of the world: you get all of the amenities of a luxury hotel and enough activities to guarantee fun, even on rainy days. All your important decisions are made long before you board. Your itinerary is set, and you know the total cost of your vacation beforehand.

Ships usually call at several ports on a single voyage but are at each for only one day. Thus, although you may be exposed to several islands, you don't get much of a feel for any one of them. To learn how to plan, choose, and book a cruise-ship voyage, consult *Fodor's FYI: Plan & Enjoy Your Cruise* (available in bookstores everywhere).

➤CRUISE LINES: **Carnival Cruise Lines** (3655 N.W. 87th Ave., Miami, FL 33178, tel. 305/599–2600 or 800/227–6482). **Celebrity Cruises** (1050 Caribbean Way, Miami, FL 33122). **Commodore/Crown Cruise Line** (4000 Hollywood Blvd., 385-S Tower, Hollywood, FL 33021, tel. 954/967–2100 or 800/832–1122). **Crystal Cruises** (2049 Century Park E, Suite 1400, Los Angeles, CA 90067, tel. 800/446–6620). **Cunard Line** (6100

Blue Lagoon Dr., Suite 400, Miami, FL 33126, tel. 800/221–4770). **Holland America Line** (300 Elliott Ave. W, Seattle, WA 98119, tel. 800/426–0327). **Norwegian Cruise Line** (95 Merrick Way, Coral Gables, FL 33134, tel. 800/327–7030). **Princess Cruises** (10100 Santa Monica Blvd., Los Angeles, CA 90067, tel. 310/553–1770 or 800/774–6237). **Radisson Seven Seas Cruises** (600 Corporate Dr., Suite 410, Fort Lauderdale, FL 33334, tel. 800/333–3333). **Regal Cruises** (300 Regal Cruises Way, Box 1329, Palmetto, FL 34220, tel. 800/270–7245). **Royal Caribbean Cruise Line** (1050 Caribbean Way, Miami, FL 33132, tel. 800/327–6700). **Seabourn Cruise Line** (6100 Blue Lagoon Dr., Suite 400, Miami, FL 33126, tel. 800/929–9391). **Shipping Cruise Services, Ltd.** (75 Valencia Ave., Coral Gables, FL 33134, tel. 800/258–2633). **Star Clippers** (4101 Salzedo St., Coral Gables, FL 33146, tel. 800/442–0551). **Windstar Cruises** (300 Elliott Ave. W, Seattle, WA 98119, tel. 206/281–3535 or 800/258–7245).

➤**ORGANIZATIONS: Cruise Lines International Association** (CLIA) 500 5th Ave., Suite 1407, New York, NY 10110, tel. 212/921–0066).

Customs & Duties

When shopping abroad, **keep receipts** for all purchases. Upon reentering the country, **be ready to show customs officials what you've bought.** If you think a duty is incorrect, appeal the assessment. If you object to the way your clearance was handled, note the inspector's badge number. In either case, first ask to see a supervisor. If the problem isn't resolved, write to the appropriate authorities, beginning with the port director at your point of entry.

IN ARUBA

You can bring up to 1 liter of spirits, 3 liters of beer, or 2.25 liters of wine per person, and up to 200 cigarettes or 20 cigars. You don't need to declare the value of gifts or other items, although customs officials may inquire about large items or large quantities of items and charge (at their discretion) an import tax of 7.5% to 22% on items worth more than $230. Meat, birds, and illegal substances are forbidden. You may be asked to provide written verification that plants are free of diseases. If you're traveling with pets, bring a veterinarian's note attesting to their good health.

➤**INFORMATION: Aruba Customs Office** (tel. 297/582–1800).

IN AUSTRALIA

Australian residents who are 18 or older may bring home A$400 worth of souvenirs and gifts (including jewelry), 250 cigarettes or 250 grams of tobacco, and 1,125 ml of alcohol (including wine, beer, and spirits). Residents under 18 may bring back A$200 worth of goods. Prohibited items include meat products. Seeds, plants, and fruits need to be declared upon arrival.

➤**INFORMATION: Australian Customs Service** (Regional Director: Box 8, Sydney, NSW 2001, tel. 02/9213–2000, fax 02/9213–4000, www.customs.gov.au).

IN CANADA

Canadian residents who have been out of Canada for at least seven days may bring in C$750 worth of goods duty-free. If you've been away fewer than seven days but more than 48 hours, the duty-free allowance drops to C$200; if your trip lasts 24 to 48 hours, the allowance is C$50. You may not pool allowances with family members. Goods claimed under the C$750 exemption may follow you by mail; those claimed under the lesser exemptions must accompany you. Alcohol and tobacco products may be included in the seven-day and 48-hour exemptions but not in the 24-hour exemption. If you meet the age requirements of the province or territory through which you reenter Canada, you may bring in, duty-free, 1.5 liters of wine or 1.14 liters (40 imperial ounces) of liquor or 24 12-ounce cans or bottles of beer or ale. If you are 19 or older you may bring in, duty-free, 200 cigarettes and 50 cigars. Check ahead of time with the Canada Customs and Revenue Agency or the Department of Agriculture for policies regarding meat products, seeds, plants, and fruits.

You may send an unlimited number of gifts (only one gift per recipient, however) worth up to C$60 each duty-free to Canada. Label the package UNSOLICITED GIFT—VALUE UNDER $60. Alcohol and tobacco are excluded.

➤INFORMATION: **Canada Customs and Revenue Agency** (2265 St. Laurent Blvd. S, Ottawa, Ontario K1G 4K3, tel. 204/983–3500, 506/636–5064, 800/461–9999 in Canada, www.ccra-adrc.gc.ca).

IN NEW ZEALAND

All homeward-bound residents may bring back NZ$700 worth of souvenirs and gifts; passengers may not pool their allowances, and children can claim only the concession on goods intended for their own use. For those 17 or older, the duty-free allowance also includes 4.5 liters of wine or beer; one 1,125-ml bottle of spirits; and either 200 cigarettes, 250 grams of tobacco, 50 cigars, or a combination of the three up to 250 grams. Meat products, seeds, plants, and fruits must be declared upon arrival to the Agricultural Services Department.

➤INFORMATION: **New Zealand Customs** (Head Office, The Customhouse: 17–21 Whitmore St., Box 2218, Wellington, tel. 09/300–5399, www.customs.govt.nz).

IN THE U.K.

From countries outside the European Union you may bring home, duty-free, 200 cigarettes or 50 cigars; 1 liter of spirits or 2 liters of fortified or sparkling wine or liqueurs; 2 liters of still table wine; 60 ml of perfume; 250 ml of toilet water; plus £145 worth of other goods, including gifts and souvenirs. Prohibited items include meat products, seeds, plants, and fruits.

➤**INFORMATION: HM Customs and Excise** (St. Christopher House, Southwark, London SE1 OTE, tel. 020/7928–3344, www.hmce.gov.uk).

IN THE U.S.

U.S. residents who have been out of the country for at least 48 hours and who have not used the $600 allowance or any part of it in the past 30 days may bring home $600 worth of foreign goods duty-free. This allowance, higher than the standard $400 exemption, applies to the 24 countries in the Caribbean Basin Initiative, including Aruba. If you visit a CBI country and a non-CBI country, you may still bring in $600 worth of goods duty-free, but no more than $400 may be from the non-CBI country. If you're returning from the U.S. Virgin Islands (USVI), the duty-free allowance is $1,200. If your travel included the USVI and another country—say, the Dominican Republic—the $1,200 allowance still applies, but at least $600 worth of goods must be from the USVI.

U.S. residents 21 and older may bring back 1 liter of alcohol duty-free. In addition, regardless of your age, you are allowed 200 cigarettes and 100 non-Cuban cigars. Antiques, which the U.S. Customs Service defines as objects more than 100 years old, enter duty-free, as do original works of art done entirely by hand, including paintings, drawings, and sculptures. You may also send packages home duty-free, with a limit of one parcel per addressee per day (except alcohol or tobacco products or perfume worth more than $5). You can mail up to $200 worth of goods for personal use; label the package PERSONAL USE and attach a list of its contents and their retail value. If the package contains your used personal belongings, mark it PERSONAL GOODS RETURNED to avoid paying duties. You may send up to $100 worth of goods as a gift; mark the package UNSOLICITED GIFT. Mailed items do not affect your duty-free allowance on your return.

➤**INFORMATION: U.S. Customs Service** (for inquiries: 1300 Pennsylvania Ave. NW, Washington, DC 20229, www.customs.

gov, tel. 202/354–1000; for complaints: Customer Satisfaction Unit, 1300 Pennsylvania Ave. NW, Room 5.5A, Washington, DC 20229; for registration of equipment: Office of Passenger Programs, 1300 Pennsylvania Ave. NW, Room 5.4D, Washington, DC 20229, tel. 202/927–0530).

Electricity

Aruba runs on a 110-volt cycle, the same as in the United States; outlets are usually the two-prong variety. Total blackouts are rare, and most large hotels have backup generators.

Emergencies

➤CONTACTS: **Air Ambulance** (tel. 297/582–9197). **Ambulance and Fire** (tel. 115). **Botica Eagle Pharmacy** (L. G. Smith Blvd., near hospital, tel. 297/587–6103). **Horacio Oduber Hospital** (L. G. Smith Blvd., across from Costa Linda Beach Resort and the Alhambra Casino, tel. 297/587–4300). **Police** (tel. 111000).

Etiquette & Behavior

It's best not to mention to residents how "American" everything is—many have settled here from South America and Europe. Aruba has a separate status with the Kingdom of the Netherlands, allowing it to handle its own aviation, customs, immigration, communications, and other internal matters, but the island does retain strong economic, cultural, and political ties with Holland.

Health

DIVERS' ALERT
Don't fly within 24 hours of scuba diving. In an emergency, Air Ambulance, run by Rupert Richard, will fly you to Curaçao at a low altitude if you need to get to a decompression chamber.

FOOD & DRINK

As a rule, water is pure and food is wholesome in hotels and local restaurants throughout Aruba, but **be cautious when buying food from street vendors.** And just as you would at home, **wash or peel all fruits and vegetables** before eating them. Traveler's diarrhea, caused by consuming contaminated water, unpasteurized milk and milk products, and unrefrigerated food, isn't a big problem—unless it happens to you. So **watch what you eat,** especially at outdoor buffets in the hot sun. Make sure cooked food is hot and cold food has been properly refrigerated.

Mild cases of diarrhea may respond to Imodium (known generically as loperamide) or Pepto-Bismol (not as strong), both of which can be purchased in local pharmacies. Drink plenty of bottled water to keep from becoming dehydrated. A salt-sugar solution (½ teaspoon salt and 4 tablespoons sugar) per quart of water is a good remedy for rehydrating yourself.

PESTS & OTHER HAZARDS

The major health risk is sunburn or sunstroke. A long-sleeve shirt, a hat, and long pants or a beach wrap are essential on a boat, for midday at the beach, and whenever you go out sightseeing. **Use sunscreen** with an SPF of at least 15—especially if you're fair—and apply it liberally on your nose, ears, and other sensitive and exposed areas. Make sure the sunscreen is waterproof if you're engaging in water sports. Always **limit your sun time** for the first few days and **drink plenty of liquids.** Limit intake of caffeine and alcohol, which hasten dehydration.

Mosquitoes and flies can be bothersome, so **pack strong repellent.** The strong trade winds are a relief in the subtropical climate, but don't hang your bathing suit on a balcony—it will probably blow away. Help Arubans conserve water and energy: turn off air-conditioning when you leave your room, and don't let water run unattended.

SHOTS & MEDICATIONS

No special shots or vaccinations are required for Caribbean destinations.

➤**HEALTH WARNINGS: National Centers for Disease Control** (CDC: National Center for Infectious Diseases, Division of Quarantine, Traveler's Health Section: 1600 Clifton Rd. NE, M/S E-03, Atlanta, GA 30333, tel. 888/232–3228, fax 888/232–3299, www.cdc.gov).

Holidays

Aruba's official holidays are New Year's Day, Good Friday, Easter Sunday, and Christmas, as well as Betico Croes Day (January 25), National Anthem and Flag Day (March 18), Queen's Day (April 30), Labor Day (May 1), and Ascension Day (May 5 in 2005, May 26 in 2006, May 17 in 2007).

Lodging

Assume that hotels operate on the **European Plan** (EP, with no meals) unless we specify that they use the **Continental Plan** (CP, with a Continental breakfast), **Modified American Plan** (MAP, with breakfast and dinner), or are **All-Inclusive** (AI).

Mail & Shipping

From Aruba to the United States or Canada, a letter costs Afl1.40 (about 80¢) and a postcard costs Afl.60 (35¢). Expect it to take one to two weeks. A letter to Europe is Afl1.50 (90¢) and a postcard is Afl.70 (40¢). It takes two to four weeks, so you'll probably make it home before your letter does. Prices to Australia and New Zealand (three to four weeks) are slightly higher. When addressing letters to Aruba, don't worry about the lack of formal addresses or postal codes; the island's postal service knows where to go.

If you need to send a package in a hurry, there are a few options to get the job done. The Federal Express office across from the airport offers overnight service to the United States if you get your package in before 3 PM. Another big courier service is UPS, and there are also several smaller local courier services that provide international deliveries, most of them open weekdays 9–5. Check the local phone book for details.

➤COURIER SERVICES: Federal Express (Browninvest Financial Center, Wayaca 31-A, Oranjestad, tel. 297/592–9039). UPS (Rockefellerstraat 3, Oranjestad, tel. 297/582–8646).

Money Matters

CURRENCY
Arubans happily accept U.S. dollars virtually everywhere. That said, there's no real need to exchange money, except for necessary pocket change (for soda machines or pay phones). The official currency is the Aruban florin (Afl), also called the guilder, which is made up of 100 cents. Silver coins come in denominations of 1, 2½, 5, 10, 25, and 50 (the square one) cents. Paper currency comes in denominations of 5, 10, 25, 50, and 100 florins.

At press time exchange rates were Afl1.77 per U.S. dollar and Afl1.34 per Canadian dollar. Stores, hotels, and restaurants converted at Afl1.80; supermarkets and gas stations at Afl1.75. The Dutch Antillean florin—used on Bonaire and Curaçao—isn't accepted here. Prices quoted throughout this book are in U.S. dollars unless otherwise noted.

ATMS
If you need fast cash, you'll find ATMs that accept international cards (and dispense cash in the local currency) at banks in Oranjestad, at the major malls, and along the roads leading to the hotel strip.

➤**BANKS: ABN/Amro Bank** (Caya G. F. Betico Croes 89, Oranjestad, tel. 297/582–1515). **Caribbean Mercantile Bank** (Caya G. F. Betico Croes 5, Oranjestad, tel. 297/582–3118).

CREDIT CARDS & TRAVELER'S CHECKS

Major credit cards are widely accepted at hotels, restaurants, shops, car-rental agencies, and other service providers throughout Aruba. The only places that might not accept them are open-air markets or tiny shops in out-of-the-way villages.

It's smart to **write down the number of the credit cards you're carrying** and the toll-free number to call in case the card is lost or stolen.

Throughout this guide the following abbreviations are used: **AE,** American Express; **D,** Discover; **DC,** Diners Club; **MC,** MasterCard; and **V,** Visa.

SERVICE CHARGES, TIPPING & TAXES

Hotels usually add an 11% service charge to the bill and collect 8% in government taxes for a whopping total of 19% on top of quoted rates. Restaurants generally include a 10%–15% service charge on the bill; when in doubt, ask. If service isn't included, a 10% tip is standard; if it is included, it's still customary to add something extra, usually small change, at your discretion. Taxi drivers expect a 10%–15% tip, but it isn't mandatory. Porters and bellhops should receive about $2 per bag; chambermaids about $2 a day, but check to see if their tips are included in your bill so you don't overpay. The airport departure tax is $34.50, but the fee is usually included in your ticket price. Children under two don't pay departure tax. For purchases you'll pay a 6.5% ABB tax (a value-added tax) in all but the duty-free shops.

TRAVELER'S CHECKS

Get traveler's checks in small denominations—$20 or $50. Restaurants and most shops will accept them (with I.D.), and your hotel will cash them for you, though you might get change in local currency. In rural areas and small villages you'll need cash. Lost or stolen checks can usually be replaced within 24 hours. **Buy and pay for your own traveler's checks;** the person who bought the checks must request the refund.

Packing

Dress on Aruba is generally casual. **Bring loose-fitting clothing made of natural fabrics** to see you through days of heat and humidity. **Pack a beach cover-up,** both to protect yourself from the sun and to provide something to wear to and from your hotel room. Bathing suits and immodest attire are frowned upon away from the beach. A sun hat is advisable, but you don't have to pack one—inexpensive straw hats are available everywhere. For shopping and sightseeing, bring walking shorts, jeans, T-shirts, long-sleeve cotton shirts, slacks, and sundresses. Nighttime dress can range from very informal to casually elegant, depending on the establishment. A tie is practically never required, but a jacket may be appropriate in fancy restaurants. You may need a light sweater or jacket for evenings.

In your carry-on luggage, **pack an extra pair of eyeglasses or contact lenses** (but if you forget, there are several eye-care centers in town where you can pick up a spare pair of lenses) and **enough of any medication you take** to last the entire trip. You may also ask your doctor to write a spare prescription using the drug's generic name, since brand names may vary from country to country. In luggage to be checked, **never pack prescription drugs or valuables.** To avoid customs delays, carry medications in their original packaging. And don't forget to carry with you the addresses of offices that handle refunds of lost traveler's checks.

CHECKING LUGGAGE

You are allowed one carry-on bag and one personal article, such as a purse or a laptop computer. Make sure that everything you carry aboard will fit under your seat or in the overhead bin. Get to the gate early, so you can board as soon as possible, before the overhead bins fill up.

If you are flying internationally, note that baggage allowances may be determined not by piece but by weight—generally 88 pounds (40 kilograms) in first class, 66 pounds (30 kilograms) in business class, and 44 pounds (20 kilograms) in economy.

Before departure, **itemize your bags' contents** and their worth, and label the bags with your name, address, and phone number. (If you use your home address, cover it so potential thieves can't see it readily.) Inside each bag, **pack a copy of your itinerary.** At check-in, **make sure that each bag is correctly tagged** with the destination airport's three-letter code. If your bags arrive damaged or fail to arrive at all, file a written report with the airline before leaving the airport.

Passports

When traveling internationally, **carry your passport** even if you don't need one (it's always the best form of I.D.) and **make two photocopies of the data page** (one for someone at home and another for you, carried separately from your passport). If you lose your passport, promptly call the nearest embassy or consulate and the local police.

U.S. passport applications for children under age 14 require consent from both parents or legal guardians; both parents must appear together to sign the application. If only one parent appears, he or she must submit a written statement from the other parent authorizing passport issuance for the child. A parent with sole authority must present evidence of it when applying; acceptable documentation includes the child's certified birth certificate listing only the applying parent, a court order specifically permitting this parent's travel with the child, or a death certificate for the nonapplying parent. Application forms and instructions are available on the Web site of the U.S. State Department's Bureau of Consular Affairs, www.travel. state.gov.

ENTERING ARUBA

U.S. and Canadian citizens need a valid passport or a birth certificate with a raised seal and a government-issued photo I.D. Visitors from the member countries of the European Union must also carry their European Union Travel Card, as well as a passport. All other nationalities must have a valid passport.

PASSPORT OFFICES

The best time to apply for a passport or to renew is in fall and winter. Before any trip check your passport's expiration date and, if necessary, renew it as soon as possible.

➤**AUSTRALIAN CITIZENS: Australian Passport Office** (tel. 131–232, www.dfat.gov.au/passports).

➤**CANADIAN CITIZENS: Passport Office** (tel. 819/994–3500 or 800/567–6868, www.dfait-maeci.gc.ca/passport).

➤**NEW ZEALAND CITIZENS: New Zealand Passport Office** (tel. 04/494–0700, www.passports.govt.nz).

➤**U.K. CITIZENS: London Passport Office** (tel. 0990/210–410) for fees and documentation requirements and for an emergency passport.

➤**U.S. CITIZENS: National Passport Information Center** (tel. 900/225–5674) calls are 35¢ per minute for automated service, $1.05 per minute for operator service.

Rest Rooms

Outside of Oranjestad, the only public rest rooms you'll find will be in one of the few restaurants that dot the countryside.

Safety

Arubans are very friendly, so you needn't be afraid to stop and ask anyone for directions. It's a relatively safe island, but commonsense rules still apply. Lock your rental car when you leave it, and leave valuables in your hotel safe. Don't leave bags unattended in the airport, on the beach, or on tour vehicles.

Shopping

For many, shopping on Aruba means duty-free bargains on jewelry, designer clothing, china, crystal, and other luxury goods from around the world. At the Aruba Trading Company in the airport departure hall (near U.S. immigration), you'll find a complete selection of duty-free liquors, tobacco, and perfumes. For others, shopping means buying locally produced crafts and works of art.

Bargaining isn't expected in shops, but at open-air markets and with street vendors it may be acceptable. Keep in mind, however, that selling handicrafts or homegrown produce may be a local's only livelihood. When bargaining, consider the amount of work or effort involved and the item's value to you. Vendors don't set artificially high prices and then expect to bargain; they bargain so you'll buy from them instead of their neighbor.

Taxis

There's a dispatch office at the airport; you can also flag down taxis on the street (look for license plates with a "TX" tag). Rates are fixed (i.e., there are no meters; the rates are set by the government and displayed on a chart), though you and the driver should agree on the fare before your ride begins. Add $1 to the fare after midnight and $1–$3 on Sunday and holidays. An hour-long island tour costs about $30, with up to four people.

Rides into town from Eagle Beach run about $5; from Palm Beach, about $8.

➤TAXI SERVICE: **Airport Taxi Dispatch** (tel. 297/582–2116).

Telephones

To call Aruba direct from the United States, dial 011–297, followed by the seven-digit number in Aruba. (To call from elsewhere abroad, substitute the country of origin's international access code for the 011.) International, direct, and operator-assisted calls from Aruba to all countries in the world are possible via hotel operators or from the Government Long Distance Telephone, Telegraph, and Radio Office (SETAR), in the post-office building in Oranjestad. When making calls on Aruba, simply dial the seven-digit number. AT&T customers can dial 800–8000 from special phones at the cruise dock and in the airport's arrival and departure halls. From other phones dial 121 to contact the SETAR international operator to place a collect or AT&T calling-card call. Local calls from pay phones, which accept both local currency and phone cards, cost 25¢. Business travelers or vacationers who need to be in regular contact with their families at home can rent an international cell phone from the concierge in most hotels or at some local electronics stores.

Tours & Packages

Because everything is prearranged on a prepackaged tour or independent vacation, you spend less time planning—and often get it all at a good price.

BOOKING WITH AN AGENT

Travel agents are excellent resources. But it's a good idea to collect brochures from several agencies, as some agents' suggestions may be influenced by relationships with tour and package firms that reward them for volume sales. If you have a special interest, **find an agent with expertise in that area**; the

American Society of Travel Agents (ASTA; ☞ Travel Agencies) has a database of specialists worldwide.

Make sure your travel agent knows the accommodations and other services of the place being recommended. Ask about the hotel's location, room size, beds, and whether it has a pool, room service, or programs for children, if you care about these. Has your agent been there in person or sent others whom you can contact?

Do some homework on your own, too: local tourism boards can provide information about lesser-known and small-niche operators, some of which may sell only direct.

BUYER BEWARE

Each year consumers are stranded or lose their money when tour operators—even large ones with excellent reputations—go out of business. So **check out the operator.** Ask several travel agents about its reputation, and try to **book with a company that has a consumer-protection program.** (Look for information in the company's brochure.) In the United States, members of the National Tour Association and the United States Tour Operators Association are required to set aside funds to cover your payments and travel arrangements in the event that the company defaults. It's also a good idea to choose a company that participates in the American Society of Travel Agents' Tour Operator Program (TOP); ASTA will act as mediator in any disputes between you and your tour operator.

Remember that the more your package or tour includes the better you can predict the ultimate cost of your vacation. Make sure you know exactly what is covered, and **beware of hidden costs.** Are taxes, tips, and transfers included? Entertainment and excursions? These can add up.

▶**TOUR-OPERATOR RECOMMENDATIONS: American Society of Travel Agents** (☞ Travel Agencies). **National Tour Association** (NTA) 546 E. Main St., Lexington, KY 40508, tel.

859/226–4444 or 800/682–8886, www.ntaonline.com). **United States Tour Operators Association** (USTOA) 275 Madison Ave., Suite 2014, New York, NY 10016, tel. 212/599–6599 or 800/ 468–7862, fax 212/599–6744, www.ustoa.com).

ISLAND TOURS

If you try a cruise around the island, know that the choppy waters are stirred up by trade winds and that catamarans are much smoother than single-hulled boats. Sucking on a peppermint or lemon candy may help a queasy stomach; avoid boating with an empty or overly full stomach. Moonlight cruises cost about $25 per person. There are also snorkeling, dinner and dancing, and sunset party cruises to choose from, priced from $25 to $60 per person. Many of the smaller operators work out of their homes; they often offer to pick you up (and drop you off) at your hotel or meet you at a particular hotel pier.

Explore an underwater reef teeming with marine life without getting wet. Atlantis Submarines operates a 65-foot air-conditioned sub that takes 48 passengers 95–150 feet below the surface along Barcadera Reef. The two-hour trip (including boat transfer to the submarine platform and 50-minute plunge) costs $72. Make reservations one day in advance. Another option is the *Seaworld Explorer*, a semisubmersible that allows you to view Aruba's marine habitat from 6 feet below the surface. The cost is $35 for a 1½-hour tour.

You can see the main sights in one day, but set aside two days to really meander. Guided tours are your best option if you have only a short time. Aruba's Transfer Tour & Taxi C.A. takes you to the main sights on personalized tours that cost $30 per hour.

De Palm Tours has a near monopoly on Aruban sightseeing; you can make reservations through its general office or at hotel tour-desk branches. The company's basic 3½-hour tour hits the highlights. Wear tennis or hiking shoes, and bring a lightweight jacket or wrap (the air-conditioned bus gets cold). It begins at

9:30 AM, picks you up in your hotel lobby, and costs $22.50 per person. A full-day Jeep Adventure tour ($59.50 per person) takes you to sights that would be difficult for you to find on your own. Bring a bandanna to cover your mouth; the ride on rocky dirt roads can get dusty. De Palm also offers full-day tours of Curaçao ($219; every Friday). Prices include round-trip airfare, transfers, sightseeing, and lunch; there's free time for shopping.

Romantic horse-drawn-carriage rides through the city streets of Oranjestad run $30 for a 30-minute tour; hours of operation are 7 PM–11 PM, and carriages depart from the clock tower at the Royal Plaza Mall.

➤**BOAT TOUR OPERATORS: Atlantis Submarines** (Seaport Village Marina, tel. 297/583–6090). **De Palm Tours** (L. G. Smith Blvd. 142, Oranjestad, tel. 297/582–4400 or 800/766–6016, www.depalm.com). **Pelican Tours & Watersports** (J. E. Irausquin Blvd. 232, Oranjestad, tel. 297/587–2302, www.pelican-aruba.com). **Red Sail Sports** (Seaport Village Mall, L. G. Smith Blvd. 82, Oranjestad, tel. 297/586–1603, 877/733–7245 in the U.S., www.aruba-redsail.com). **Seaworld Explorer** (tel. 297/586–2416).

➤**ORIENTATION TOUR OPERATORS: Aruba's Transfer Tour & Taxi** (Pos Abao 41, Oranjestad, tel. 297/582–2116). **De Palm Tours** (L. G. Smith Blvd. 142, Oranjestad, tel. 297/582–4400 or 800/766–6016, www.depalm.com).

Travel Agencies

A good travel agent puts your needs first. Look for an agency that has been in business at least five years, emphasizes customer service, and has someone on staff who specializes in your destination. In addition, **make sure the agency belongs to a professional trade organization.** The American Society of Travel Agents (ASTA)—the largest and most influential in the field with more than 24,000 members in some 140 countries—maintains and enforces a strict code of ethics and will step in to help mediate any agent-client disputes involving ASTA members if necessary. ASTA (whose motto is "Without a travel agent, you're on your own") also maintains a Web site that includes a directory of agents. (If a travel agency is also acting as your tour operator, *see* Buyer Beware in Tours & Packages.)

➤**LOCAL AGENT REFERRALS: American Society of Travel Agents** (ASTA) 1101 King St., Suite 200, Alexandria, VA 22314, tel. 800/965–2782 24-hr hot line, fax 703/739–3268, www.astanet.com). **Association of British Travel Agents** (68–71 Newman St., London W1T 3AH, tel. 020/7637–2444, fax 020/7637–0713, www.abtanet.com). **Association of Canadian Travel Agents** (130 Albert St., Suite 1705, Ottawa, Ontario K1P 5G4, tel. 613/237–3657, fax 613/237–7052, www.acta.net). **Australian Federation of Travel Agents** (Level 3, 309 Pitt St., Sydney, NSW 2000, tel. 02/9264–3299, fax 02/9264–1085, www.afta.com.au). **Travel Agents' Association of New Zealand** (Level 5, Tourism and Travel House, 79 Boulcott St., Box 1888, Wellington 10033, tel. 04/499–0104, fax 04/499–0827, www.taanz.org.nz).

Time

Aruba is in the Atlantic Standard Time zone, which is one hour later than Eastern Standard Time or four hours earlier than Greenwich mean time. During daylight saving time, between April and October, Atlantic Standard is the same time as Eastern Daylight Time.

Visitor Information

Before leaving home, contact the Aruba Tourism Authority at one of its many offices. On Aruba the tourist office has free brochures and information officers who are ready to answer any questions you may have, weekdays 7:30 AM–4:30 PM.

The Caribbean Tourism Organization, which has information on the island, is another good resource.

➤**ARUBA INFORMATION: Aruba Tourism Authority** (tel. 800/862–7822, www.arubatourism.com; L. G. Smith Blvd. 172, Eagle Beach, Aruba, tel. 297/582–3777; 1 Financial Plaza, Suite 136, Fort Lauderdale, FL 33394, tel. 954/767–6477; 3455 Peach Tree Rd. NE, Suite 500, Atlanta, GA 30326, tel. 404/892–7822; 5901 N. Cicero, Suite 301, Chicago, IL, 60646, tel. 773/202–5054; 1000 Harbor Blvd., Ground Level, Weehawken, NJ 07087, tel. 201/330–0800; 12707 North Freeway, Suite 138, Houston, TX 77060-1234, tel. 281/872–7822; Business Centre 5875, Suite 201, Hwy. 7, Vaughan, Ontario, L4L 8Z7, tel. 905/264–3434).

➤**CARIBBEAN-WIDE INFORMATION: Caribbean Tourism Organization** (80 Broad St., New York, NY 10004, tel. 212/635–9530, www.caribtourism.com; Vigilant House, 120 Wilton Rd., London SW1V 1JZ, tel. 020/7233–8382).

➤**U.S. GOVERNMENT ADVISORIES: U.S. Department of State** (Overseas Citizens Services Office, Room 4811 N.S., 2201 C St. NW, Washington, DC 20520, tel. 202/647–5225 for interactive hotline, 301/946–4400 computer bulletin board, fax 202/647–3000 interactive hot line); enclose a self-addressed, stamped business-size envelope.

Web Sites

Do check out the World Wide Web when you're planning. You'll find everything from up-to-date weather forecasts to virtual tours of famous cities. Fodor's Web site, www.fodors.com., is a great place to start your online travels.

One of the most helpful sites about Aruba may very well be the island's own www.aruba.com. For information on the Caribbean, visit one of the following: www.doitcaribbean.com (the Caribbean Tourism Organization's official site, with many island-specific links); www.caribbeanchannel.com (with information presented both thematically and by island); www.caribbeantravel. com (the official Caribbean Hotel Association site); www. caribbeancyberspace.com (for general information and good links); www.caribbeannewspapers.com (with links to newspapers published throughout the Caribbean); www.caribinfo.com (with a directory of Web sites based in or related to the Caribbean and links to local phone directories); www.cruising.org (the Cruise Lines International Association's site, with many ship profiles); www.cananews.com and www.cweek.com (for Caribbean news).

Weddings

One of the biggest concerns when planning a wedding in the Caribbean is the weather. Storms can be an obstacle in getting to the island and can batter that beautiful location. Not so in Aruba. Located outside the hurricane belt, the island enjoys a consistently dry climate, with temperatures around 80°F every day of the year.

In 2002, the Aruba Parliament passed a law enabling people over the age of 18 to marry as long as they submit the appropriate documents 14 days in advance. Couples are required to submit birth certificates with raised seals, through the mail or in person, to Aruba's Office of the Civil Registry. They also need an apostil—a document proving they are free to marry—from their country of residence.

With so many beautiful spots to choose from, weddings on Aruba are guaranteed to be romantic. The island's endless beaches are a natural, but other choices include the tropical gardens at Arikok National Park, the top of Natural Bridge, or a sunset cruise. And be sure to register for the island's "One Cool Honeymoon" program for special discounts from local businesses. Ask your hotel for more information.

Aruba Weddings For You is a small company that helps couples make wedding arrangements in advance. Services include securing a location on the island, submitting legal documents, confirming arrangements with suppliers, decorating the venue, and coordinating the ceremony. You can also check out Aruba Fairy Tales, another company that arranges weddings.

➤INFORMATION: Aruba Fairy Tales (Box 4151, Noord, tel. 297/993–0045, fax 297/583–1511, www.arubafairytales.com). Aruba Weddings For You (Nune 92, Paradera, tel. 297/583–7638, fax 297/588–6073, www.arubaweddingsforyou.com).

When to Go

Aruba's high season is traditionally winter—from December 15 to April 14—when northern weather is at its worst. During this season you're guaranteed the most entertainment at resorts and the most people with whom to enjoy it. It's also the most fashionable, the most expensive, and the most popular time to visit—and most hotels are heavily booked. You must make reservations at least two or three months in advance for the very best places. Hotel prices drop 20%–40% after April 15; cruise prices also fall.

➤FORECASTS: **Weather Channel Connection** (tel. 900/932–8437), 95¢ per minute from a Touch-Tone phone.

index

FODOR'S POCKET ARUBA

EDITOR: Mark Sullivan

Editorial Contributors: Karen W. Bressler, Suzanne Bressler, and Elise Rosen

Editorial Production: Jenna L. Bagnini

Maps: David Lindroth, *cartographer;* Bob Blake and Rebecca Baer, *map editors*

Design: Fabrizio La Rocca, *creative director;* Tigist Getachew, *art director*

Production/Manufacturing: Angela L. McLean

Cover Photograph: Darrell Jones/AllStock/PictureQuest

COPYRIGHT

Third Edition

ISBN 1-4000-1409-3

ISSN 1098-2663

IMPORTANT TIP

Although all prices, opening times, and other details in this book are based on information supplied to us at press time, changes occur all the time in the travel world, and Fodor's cannot accept responsibility for facts that become outdated or for inadvertent errors or omissions. So **always confirm information when it matters,** especially if you're making a detour to visit a specific place.

SPECIAL SALES

This book is available for special discounts for bulk purchases for sales promotions or premiums. Special editions, including personalized covers, excerpts of existing books, and corporate imprints, can be created in large quantities for special needs. For more information, write to Special Markets/Premium Sales, 1745 Broadway, MD 6-2, New York, New York 10019, or e-mail specialmarkets@randomhouse.com.

PRINTED IN THE UNITED STATES OF AMERICA

10 9 8 7 6 5 4 3 2 1